Against the Tide

DATE DUE

Against the Tide

Household Structure, Opportunities, and Outcomes among White and Minority Youth

Carolyn J. Hill
Harry J. Holzer
Henry Chen

2009

W.E. Upjohn Institute for Employment Research
Kalamazoo, Michigan

Library of Congress Cataloging-in-Publication Data

Hill, Carolyn J.
  Against the tide : household structure, opportunities, and outcomes among white and minority youth / Carolyn J. Hill, Harry J. Holzer, Henry Chen.
    p. cm.
  Includes bibliographical references.
  ISBN-13: 978-0-88099-341-8 (pbk. : alk. paper)
  ISBN-10: 0-88099-341-3 (pbk. : alk. paper)
  ISBN-13: 978-0-88099-342-5 (hardcover : alk. paper)
  ISBN-10: 0-88099-342-1 (hardcover : alk. paper)
  1. Minority youth—United States. 2. Households—United States. 3. Discrimination in employment—United States. I. Holzer, Harry J., 1957- II. Chen, Henry. III. Title.

HQ796.H4877 2009
306.85'608900973—dc22

                    2008052070

Cover design by Alcorn Publication Design.
Index prepared by Diane Worden.
Printed in the United States of America.
Printed on recycled paper.

Contents

Figures

Tables

Acknowledgments

We would like to thank the Smith Richardson Foundation and the W.E. Upjohn Institute for Employment Research for generous funding of the research presented here. At the Upjohn Institute, Kevin Hollenbeck and three anonymous referees gave us detailed comments that were very helpful as we revised the manuscript. Seminar participants at the Bureau of Labor Statistics, the Upjohn Institute, the Center on Law and Social Policy, and the Association of Public Policy and Management (especially our discussant Greg Acs) gave us very helpful comments as well. Igor Kheyfets provided excellent research assistance. Finally, we want to thank Frank Furstenberg, who discussed our ideas and findings with us at various stages of this research, providing his insights along with his usual grace and good humor.

1
Introduction

Among young adults in the United States, employment and educational outcomes (such as wages, weeks worked, enrollment in college, and educational attainment) are lower for minorities, and especially for African Americans, than for whites. These gaps have been persistent over time and in some cases are expanding. Among young black men, employment outcomes are growing worse, falling behind even those of young black women. High rates of crime and incarceration, and high levels of teen pregnancy and unmarried parenthood, persist as well.

Why does a continuing gap exist between minority young adults—especially black young adults—and their white counterparts, and why are some gaps actually widening over time? One possibility involves the increasing number of youth who have grown up in single-parent households. The proportion of young blacks growing up in female-headed households increased dramatically in the 1970s and 1980s; this, in turn, might help explain why black male youth and young adults today have experienced worsening employment outcomes, rising incarceration, and increasing single parenthood.

In this monograph, we examine the effects of household structure on young adults and how these effects might have contributed to some of the negative trends we have observed for minorities (and especially blacks) over time. We do not examine the causes of growing single parenthood, especially in the black community. These causes likely include the many other causes of deteriorating employment outcomes and high incarceration rates of less-educated men in general, and black men in particular, as well as other factors (including many changes in social norms, attitudes, and behaviors) that all limit young black males' potential and their attractiveness as marriage partners. Understanding these causes is crucial to developing any policy response that might attempt to affect patterns of household formation. Still, for the purposes of this study, we take the trends in household structure as a given and try to better understand the effects of household structure on young people growing up in these households.

While a large literature examines the effects of single parenthood on children, it generally does not focus on different effects of single-parent households by youth race and gender, nor does it tend to focus on the extent to which different trends in education, employment, unmarried childbearing, and crime across these groups might be attributable to changes in household structure. The existing studies are also largely based on data sources from the 1970s and 1980s rather than on more recent data.

In addition to examining links between household structure and outcomes, we hope to better understand the mechanisms or pathways through which growing up in a single-parent household might affect youth outcomes, and what other related factors might either reinforce or counteract these effects. For instance, the children of single mothers might be hurt by a loss of family income, a reduction in parental supervision or contact time, a lack of productive male role modeling, and other kinds of stress and instability associated with single-parent families. Because of their lower income, children in single-parent families are also more likely to live in poorer neighborhoods and attend lower-quality schools.

On the other hand, perhaps the negative effects of single parenthood can be offset to some extent by better income supports, enrichment activities in childhood, access to safer neighborhoods, more effective parenting practices on the part of the custodial parent, or by positive involvement by the absent father or other family members. We explore the extent to which some of these offsets are found in minority and especially African American families, and whether they positively influence both young males and young females in those families.

We use the National Longitudinal Survey of Youth (NLSY), and particularly data from the 1997 cohort, to address these questions. This survey collects a rich array of information about sample members, including educational, employment, crime, and fertility outcomes, the structure of households, and characteristics and behaviors of the youths' parents. Furthermore, the survey collects information about a wide variety of youths' attitudes and engagement in risky behaviors, as well as characteristics of their schools and neighborhoods.

Using the 1979 and 1997 cohorts of the NLSY, we first document changes over time in outcomes related to education, employment, and risky behaviors. We show summary data on additional outcomes available in the NLSY97 and estimate regressions for select employment and educational outcomes.

Next, we focus on data from the 1997 cohort and examine a wider range of outcomes—including marriage, fertility, and incarceration—and compute the extent to which differences in outcomes across racial groups can be accounted for by differences in the household structures under which children grew up, as well as differences in family income. In addition to ordinary least squares (OLS) regressions, we estimate individual and sibling fixed-effects models to explore whether effects of household structure are likely causal.

Then we examine mediating variables through which single parenthood might affect youth outcomes, including parenting behaviors and reduced supervision time or parental contact with youth. Other factors that might be correlated with single parenthood—such as less stimulating home environments and less stable or secure neighborhoods in which young people reside—are considered here as well. Finally, we sum up our findings and consider their broad implications for policy.

We find that young people growing up in single-parent families face a combination of additional challenges that they must overcome in order to succeed. In addition to lower family incomes, they grow up in families with younger and less-educated mothers, in less stimulating environments, and in less secure neighborhoods. Some of these factors are likely caused, as least to some extent, by the single parenthood of their mothers; others are not. It is as if these young people must swim against the tide, facing fewer opportunities and many more challenges than do most young people in two-parent families in order to attain educational and employment success.

In this chapter we review previous literature on educational and employment outcomes among white and minority youth, and on household structure and its effects on outcomes. We describe our data and empirical methods in greater detail, summarize our main findings, and, finally, outline the remainder of the book.

PRIOR RESEARCH

Race/Gender Gaps in Outcomes: Education, Employment, and More

A wide variety of literature documents the continuing gaps in employment between minorities—especially African Americans—and whites, and within racial groups by gender. For example, employment rates among young, less-educated minority women—particularly African American single mothers—improved dramatically during the 1990s. These improvements are frequently attributed to the combination of a very strong economy, welfare reform, and increases in work supports for low-income parents, such as the Earned Income Tax Credit and child care subsidies (Blank 2002).

In contrast, employment rates among less-educated young white and Hispanic men declined somewhat in the 1980s and stabilized in the 1990s, while those of young black men continued to decline fairly sharply throughout this period. A relatively large literature has explored the causes of reduced employment among young black men, especially in the 1980s. This literature has focused on the labor market changes during that time that eliminated well-paying jobs for less-educated men, as well as a number of factors that affected blacks more directly than others.[1] In the 1990s, high rates of incarceration and more vigorous child support enforcement seem to have further depressed the labor market activity of this group (Holzer, Offner, and Sorensen 2005).

But why have these changes affected young black men so much more than young black women or Hispanics? Employers seem much more wary of hiring young black men than individuals from these other groups when the jobs available do not require high levels of skill; thus employers continue to discriminate in their hiring practices (Holzer 1996; Kirschenman and Neckerman 1991; Pager 2003).[2] But why these factors might have worsened over time for young black men remains unclear.

Changes in labor markets during the past two decades have raised the rewards associated with educational attainment and cognitive skills (Katz and Autor 1999), and differences in education and test scores account for large portions of the earnings gap between young whites and blacks.[3] The rate of high school completion nationally among young blacks has apparently become comparable to that of young whites, controlling for family background (Hauser 1997), but at least some of this seems to be accounted for by General Educational Development (GED) degrees, which are of lower economic value, rather than high school diplomas.[4] Administrative data from school districts also suggest much lower rates of high school completion than do self-report surveys, though some controversy remains over which is more accurate (Mishel and Roy 2006; Swanson 2004). Also, certain low-income neighborhoods in major urban areas continue to have very high dropout rates among young blacks (Orfield 2004). Rates of college attendance and completion are lower for blacks relative to whites, perhaps because of rising college costs and other factors (Ellwood and Kane 2000). Furthermore, educational attainment among young Hispanics is considerably lower than that of young whites, partly because of the presence of immigrants among the former group.

In addition, a major gender gap in college enrollments favoring women over men has developed among all ethnic groups, but especially among young minorities (Jacob 2002; Offner 2002). And test score gaps between young whites and minorities (despite some gains among the latter in the 1980s) remain quite large and are not well understood (Jencks and Phillips 1998). These gaps tend to appear quite early in life (Fryer and Levitt 2004)—mostly before children enter kindergarten— then widen in the first few years of school before stabilizing.

Other racial differences in social outcomes remain puzzling as well. Why do so many more young black men participate in crime and become incarcerated than do young people in any other race or gender group? Freeman (1996) and Grogger (1997), among others, suggest that declining wages and employment opportunities in the above-ground economy help account for the decisions of less-educated young men to engage in crime, though the sharp differences in criminal participation by race and gender may not be fully attributable to this fact alone.

Similarly, the decline in marriage rates and the rise in out-of-wedlock births among young blacks (and some Hispanics, such as Puerto Ricans) have been noteworthy. Indeed, the rise in female headship has been much steeper in black families than for other racial groups (McLanahan and Casper 1995), and it appears at least partly attributable to the declining employment and rising incarceration rates observed among young men (Blau, Kahn, and Waldfogel 2000; Lichter et al. 1992; Moffitt 2001; Wilson 1987), all of which tend to reduce their marriageability.[5]

Effects of Female Headship of Families: Blacks and Others

Has the fact that so many more young black men were growing up in lower-income female-headed families over the past few decades contributed to the greater decline in their employment and educational prospects relative to virtually every other group?

The research evidence to date strongly suggests that growing up in female-headed families appears to be harmful to youth outcomes such as graduating from high school, gaining employment, and avoiding teen pregnancy (Amato 2005; Haveman and Wolfe 1995; Hoffman, Foster, and Furstenberg 1993; Maynard 1996; McLanahan 1997; McLanahan and Sandefur 1994). Complementary findings suggest that growing up in families with married parents has positive effects on youth (Thomas and Sawhill 2002; Waite and Gallagher 2000). These findings have inspired a set of federally funded projects designed to explore the impacts of healthy marriage promotion (Lerman 2002).

Are the effects of female headship for youth and young adults more deleterious for blacks than for whites or Hispanics, or for black males than for black females? The effects of female headship on young black males might be more negative if, for example, their behaviors are more negatively affected by a lack of parental supervision, or if their attitudes and relationships are hurt by a lack of positive adult male role models and mentorship in their lives.

But little of the earlier evidence on the topic suggests that this is the case (Haurin 1992; Lee et al. 1994; McLanahan and Sandefur 1994), though much of this work is based on data from the 1970s and 1980s. In recent research, Page and Stevens (2005) find more negative effects of divorce on young blacks than whites, at least partly because of lower rates of remarriage among the former set of families. Dunifon and Kowaleski-Jones (2002) find fewer negative effects of single parenthood on young blacks than whites but more negative effects of cohabitation. But even if the estimated impacts of female headship across race and gender groups are comparable, the much greater frequency of single-parenthood in the African American community might help account for some of the less positive outcomes and trends observed among blacks in the 1980s and 1990s, especially among younger males.

Of course, the impacts of single parenthood—and the duration of time in which families find themselves in this status—might depend importantly on the extent to which the parents in these families are divorced or never married. The presence of a second parent might affect children quite differently, depending on whether the second parent is a biological or a stepparent (Acs and Nelson 2003; Lansford et al. 2001). Also, the traditional categories of being married, separated or divorced, or remarried to a stepparent may be less relevant for many low-income minority families than cohabitation: over time, single mothers seem to cohabit with one or more biological fathers of their children, and with varying frequency or duration.[6]

Are the Effects of Household Structure Causal?

In all of this literature, questions have been raised about whether these studies identify true causal effects of household structure. Estimates of the negative impacts of teen pregnancy or single parenthood and of the positive effects of marriage on both parents and children that are based on ordinary least squares (OLS) regressions may be overstated because they do not control for a set of unobserved characteristics of these parents and families that are correlated with single parenthood but not caused by it.

For instance, Geronimus and Korenman (1993) use comparisons across female siblings to argue that the negative effects of teen parenthood are mostly due to unobserved factors, such as the poorer family backgrounds of these young mothers. Rosenzweig and Wolpin (1993) incorporate comparisons across cousins as well as siblings, and also find smaller negative effects on the teen mothers and their children. Hotz, McElroy, and Sanders (1996) look at pregnant teens who successfully gave birth and compare their educational and employment outcomes to those who miscarried; they generally find smaller negative effects as well. Using sibling fixed-effects models (which control for unobservable family characteristics) with data from the NLSY79, Sandefur and Wells (1999) find that not living in a two-parent family was associated with fewer years of education completed, suggesting a causal effect of structure on educational attainment (though the magnitudes of effects are modest). And Bronars and Grogger (1994), comparing mothers of single children versus twins, suggest that some of the observed negative effects on the education and incomes of unwed mothers are causal and have long-term effects on black families.[7]

The above studies mostly focus on the teen or unwed mothers themselves, rather than on the longer-term effects on children or youth of growing up in a single-parent family. But Joyce, Kaestner, and Korenman (2000) and Korenman, Kaestner, and Joyce (2001) compare intentional versus unintentional pregnancies, among other "natural experiments," to infer the effects of unwed parenthood on outcomes of children in these families.[8] Though these researchers found that unwed pregnant women smoke more and unwed mothers breast-feed less frequently, few other negative impacts on children's test scores or behavior were observed. Similarly, Lang and Zagorsky (2001) use parental death as an instrumental variable for parental absence and find relatively few negative effects on child outcomes.

On the other hand, Gruber (2000) finds more negative effects on child outcomes from laws making it easier for parents to divorce.[9] Various studies using individual fixed effects (or "before-after" comparisons for the same individuals) to analyze the impacts of divorce on children frequently find negative effects (Morrison and Cherlin 1995; Page and Stevens 2005; Painter and Levine 2000). Ananat and Michaels (2008) use an instrumental variable strategy (with the gender of the first child as the instrument) and find strongly positive causal effects of divorce on child poverty as well, though Bedard and Deschênes (2005) find the opposite with regards to mean income.[10] But individual fixed effects will be of less value to the study of never-married mothers and their children, as single parenthood is often a permanent characteristic of these families.

While these studies raise important questions about potential biases in OLS estimates, we do not believe they have settled the issue. For instance, sibling studies have generally been based on small samples. Other studies use instrumental variables that may have limited applicability to the issue of children whose parents never married (such as the Lang-Zagorsky measure of parental death), or that may be of low quality (in terms of first-stage predictive power or true exogeneity). All of these problems could lead to potential understatement of the size or significance of the effects of growing up in a single-parent family.[11]

And, with a few exceptions (Dunifon and Kowaleski-Jones 2002; Page and Stevens 2005), the above studies do not tend to focus on differences in effects by race or gender.

Causal Pathways for Household Structure Effects

To the extent that growing up in a single-parent household has had negative effects on young blacks in recent years, why do these occur? What are the mediating variables through which these effects operate? Many scholars have noted that family incomes are reduced in single-parent families relative to two-parent families since the former have only one earner; and lower family incomes clearly affect the schooling and behavioral success of children growing up in these families (Duncan 2005). However, Mayer (1997) makes the case that other factors (such as parental attitudes and behaviors) that are heavily correlated with low incomes might actually be more important direct sources of problems for children growing up in poor families. In addition, the time constraints of single working parents might make it more difficult for them to interact with their children or to supervise their children's behavior and use of time. Financial and emotional stress on the mothers might lead to poor parenting (Kalil et al. 1998), in terms of the mothers meting out harsher punishments and getting into more conflicts with their children (Carlson and McLanahan 2002). Less orderly households might also result from these stresses on parents, which might affect children and youth negatively as well (Dunifon, Duncan, and Brooks-Gunn 2001).

Instability in living arrangements and residential locations might also contribute to poorer youth outcomes, as a stable environment might be necessary for children to develop healthy relationships and to maintain routines of productive activity (such as homework). The lower incomes and instability of single-parent families might result in less intellectually stimulating environments for children (Bradley, Caldwell, and Rock 1988) or residence in less secure neighborhoods. In addition, some of these factors might affect minority families more strongly than whites, and males in these families more severely than females—especially given the absence of positive male role models and authority figures in these families.[12]

In one well-known attempt to disentangle the negative impacts of single parenthood into these competing sources, McLanahan and Sandefur (1994) consider family income as well as "parenting variables" (such as regularity of contact with the absent father, parental assistance with homework or reading, degree of supervision and regulation of behavior, strictness of discipline, and positive aspirations) that are likely to be at least somewhat correlated with single parenthood (because of a single parent's limited time and greater stress). They also consider the frequency of residential mobility (as a measure of instability in family life that is higher for single-parent families) and quality of peers and schools. They find that lower income accounted for roughly half of the poorer outcomes of youth observed in these families. Many of the parenting and mobility variables also contribute to worse youth outcomes, though major racial and gender differences in these impacts were not found.

In an analysis of parents and youth in lower-income neighborhoods in Philadelphia, Furstenberg et al. (1999) focus on a similar set of parenting behaviors as well as various school and neighborhood factors as determinants of youth outcomes. Using an analytical framework that stresses the importance of youth development in the context of the family's school and community environment (Eccles et al. 1993; Sameroff, Seifer, and Bartko 1997), Furstenberg et al. note that even single parents in lower-income neighborhoods can encourage success among youth by "managing risk and opportunity," through either "promotive" or "preventive" strategies (or both). The promotive strategies include developing trust and healthy communication between parents and children, encouraging greater youth autonomy and participation in decision-making at home, and encouraging youth involvement in a variety of school and community organizations that might strengthen their cognitive, social, and psychological skills. In contrast, the preventive strategies entail more restrictions on youth activity out of the home, more supervision, and stronger punishments for violations of the rules.

The authors find that minority single parents and those in poorer neighborhoods have fewer resources (of time, money, and information) with which to pursue the promotive strategies, and therefore tend to fall back on preventive measures to a greater extent. They find that both sets of strategies can generate some successful outcomes among youth, but that differences in these approaches can also account for some of the variations in outcomes observed between single- and two-parent families, and between whites and minorities.

The study by Furstenberg and his colleagues focuses not only on mediating factors through which single parenthood affects outcomes, but also on a range of parental behaviors that can either offset or reinforce whatever disadvantages single-parent families have in income levels and quality of school or neighborhood. The extent to which their findings can be replicated in broader nationwide data, covering a much wider range of youth outcomes in school and in the labor market, needs to be examined.

The special developmental needs of young black males, and the kinds of mentoring and education/training programs that address these needs, have also received some attention (e.g., Mincy 1994). Clayton, Mincy, and Blankenhorn (2003) have also recently focused on fatherhood among black men and have considered how more positive parenting can be encouraged both within marriage and among black noncustodial fathers.[13] But the extent to which specific parenting behaviors among noncustodial black fathers are associated with improved educational and employment outcomes among their sons and daughters has not been explored systematically.

Preliminary Studies Using the NLSY97

The potential usefulness of the NLSY97 in addressing these many questions is discussed below. But some new evidence on this topic, and the richness of the data on youth and their families (even relative to the earlier 1979 cohort of the NLSY and other data sets), was highlighted in a volume of papers (Michael 2001) and in a special issue of the *Journal of Human Resources* (JHR 2001). Using the NLSY97, the papers in those volumes provide an early snapshot of young people aged 12–16, and of the important influences of family background and environment on their own attitudes and behaviors. In particular, Pierret (2001) found strong effects of family structure on grades, tendency to use alcohol and drugs, and participation in crime; Moore (2001) found similar effects on adolescent sexual behavior, and Tepper (2001) found major effects of parental regulations on adolescent use of time. At that point, though, few data were available in the NLSY97 that allowed a study of the determinants of educational and employment outcomes (instead of just youths' expectations of these outcomes), as well as marriage, fertility, crime, and other outcomes.

Summary

A lengthy literature strongly suggests that single parenthood has negative consequences for the educational, employment, and behavioral outcomes of young people growing up in these households. But many important questions remain unanswered. In particular, we still know relatively little about the extent to which growing single parenthood among minorities, and especially among blacks, can help account for poor educational, employment, marital, pregnancy, and crime outcomes among young adults—and even among black males relative to black females. The extent to which previous estimates of the impacts of household structure on young adult educational and employment outcomes are causal remains uncertain, as are the exact mechanisms through which household structure might have its effects. Generating answers to these questions can provide insight into developing appropriate policies to help young minorities improve their educational and employment outcomes in the future.

RESEARCH QUESTIONS

In this monograph, we address the following questions:

1) What are the trends over time in employment, education, single parenthood, and participation in risky behaviors for young adults, overall and separately by race and gender?

2) What are the effects of growing up in a single-parent home on outcomes related to education, employment, unmarried parenthood, and incarceration for young adults overall, as well as separately for young black men and young black women? Has the growth of single parenthood, especially female headship in black families, contributed to growing gaps in education and employment for black male youth and young adults relative to other males, and to gaps between black males and black females?

3) Are the observed effects of growing up in a single-parent home causal, or do the effects reflect other factors that are correlated both with growing up in a single-parent home and with young-adult outcomes?

4) To the extent that growing up in a single-parent home affects youth and young-adult outcomes, why does it do so? Do its effects work primarily through reduced income or through other parenting behaviors and instability? To what extent does it work through quality of the home and neighborhood environment (which may or may not be causally related to single parenthood per se)? Do these patterns vary by race and gender?

DATA AND METHODS

To answer these questions, we analyze data from the National Longitudinal Survey of Youth (NLSY). We focus on the 1997 cohort (NLSY97), a nationally representative sample of about 9,000 youths who were ages 12 to 16 at the end of December 1996. Our analysis uses the first eight panels of data, allowing us to observe this cohort in early adulthood (ages 20 to 24). To provide a comparative perspective over time on our research questions, we also use an earlier cohort, the NLSY79, a panel survey that has followed more than 12,000 young men and women who were 14 to 21 years old at the end of 1978.

Using the extensive data available in the NLSY, we estimate the effects of growing up in a single-parent home on a wide variety of young-adult outcomes, separately by race and gender. Although we focus on the NLSY97 cohort, we generate estimates of outcomes using both the 1979 and 1997 cohorts to document changes over time for different race-gender groups.

Our goal is to examine a wide variety of outcomes of youth and young adults that might be affected by growing up with single parents. As Acs (2006) notes, the range of outcomes potentially affected might be grouped into three categories: cognitive, school-based, and behavioral.[14] All of these outcomes might ultimately affect other measures of individual success, especially earnings and employment.

The NLSY97 contains a wealth of information for measuring the outcomes and explanatory measures in our study. As an overview, these data provide detailed evidence on youths' behaviors and attitudes with regard to education, employment, marriage, fertility, sexual activity, criminal activity, and risky behaviors (e.g., the use of alcohol or drugs).[15] The survey also includes extensive information on the youths' living situations and parental characteristics, including education, income, marital status, attitudes, and rule-setting behaviors (from the survey of a parent or parental figure in the first round of the survey, as well as from the youth respondent).

With regard to educational outcomes of interest, the survey contains information on enrollment status, level of schooling completed, grade point averages, and scores on the Armed Services Vocational Aptitude Battery (ASVAB).

With regard to employment outcomes of interest, information is available about all spells of employment (as an employee, a self-employed worker, or a freelancer) since the age of 12, and about the wages and other characteristics of each job.

With regard to marriage, sexual behavior, and fertility, the survey collects information on the dates of all sample members' cohabiting relationships, marriages, and disruptions or dissolution of these relationships, and on the number of pregnancies, live, and nonlive births.

Finally, with regard to criminal outcomes and other risky behaviors, the survey collects self-reported information on arrests and convictions for various crimes, as well as use of alcohol, cigarettes, and drugs. It can also gauge incarceration based on whether the interview in any particular year took place in a jail or prison facility.

The NLSY97 contains an equally rich supply of explanatory variables for these outcomes. In addition to key measures of race, ethnicity, and gender for each sample member, a strength of the data set is the availability of measures of family structure—our primary explanatory variable of interest—for the youth. We can distinguish whether the sample member was in a household with both biological parents, a single-parent household, or another type of family structure.

The survey contains extensive detail about other characteristics of the youths' parents, families, households, and nonresident relatives. These characteristics, which include parents' age, education, employment, and income, constitute a core set of explanatory control variables in our statistical models. Other measures of parental attitudes and behaviors, and of household characteristics, are included as mediators of the effects of household structure, or as reinforcing or offsetting factors of growing up in a single-parent household. Such information on parental child rearing actions and attitudes is gleaned through questions to the parent respondent in the survey's first round, as well as to the youth respondent in the first and subsequent rounds.[16]

The NLSY97 survey design restricted the sample universe for selected survey questions, and we use some of these questions in our analysis. For example, some questions about parenting behaviors and relationships were only asked of youth who were 12 to 14 years old at the end of December 1996. This sample restriction should not limit the analysis in a meaningful way. As a whole, the NLSY97 contains rich detail on youth outcomes, youth characteristics, family structure and other characteristics, parental characteristics, and other aspects of the youth's environment for analyzing the research question of how family structure influences a range of youth and young adult outcomes.

As for the empirical work and methods we will use, we first document trends in education, employment, and other behavioral outcomes by race and gender over the period of the 1980s and 1990s, using data from the two NLSY cohorts. We will especially highlight continuing gaps in outcomes by race and gender that appear in the most recent NLSY data.

Then, using the NLSY97 data, we present estimates from reduced-form equations for outcomes of interest related to education, employment, unwed parenthood, and incarceration. We focus on the effects of household structure (measured at age 12) on these outcomes, controlling for a number of sample member and maternal characteristics. These equations are estimated without and then with controls for family income, as this is one of the clearest mechanisms through which single parenthood might affect observed outcomes for youth.

To deal with issues of causality and unobserved personal characteristics, we estimate both individual and sibling fixed-effects models, in which the former focus on changes over time in individual circumstances while the latter focus on differences across sibling pairs. These methods use smaller samples, limiting our ability to produce separate estimates by youth race and gender.[17] Still, these models may produce something closer to causal estimates of the effects of household structure.

We next explore how effects of household structure are mediated through household and parental characteristics and behaviors. Following McLanahan and Sandefur (1994), Furstenberg et al. (1999), and others, we add a set of variables that may be correlated with household structure. Such measures include the degree to which the home environment provides an "enriching environment" (defined as the home usually having a computer, usually having a dictionary, and whether the youth take extra classes or lessons such as dance or music) or the quality of the neighborhood in which the youth and his or her family live. We will also consider measures of parenting styles and quality (such as parental knowledge of whom these young people spend time with when not at home) or household stability and routine as other potential mechanisms. Our goal in estimating these equations is to explore some of the mediating factors that prior research has identified as potentially important in accounting for the observed effects of household structure on youth outcomes, or that might tend to offset or exacerbate those effects in various situations.

OUTLINE OF THE REMAINDER OF THE VOLUME

In Chapter 2, we document changes in both employment and educational outcomes between the 1979 and 1997 cohorts of the NLSY, with a particular emphasis on how these trends differ across race and gender groups. We also present summary data on engagement in risky behaviors from both cohorts, but especially from the 1997 cohort. The chapter concludes with results from a set of estimated recursive equations in which educational outcomes (in particular, dropping out of high school) are related to a range of personal and behavioral characteristics, all of which are then used to explain employment outcomes for NLSY97 sample members in 2004–2005.

In Chapter 3, we begin our exploration of the effects of household structure on youth outcomes, using the NLSY97 data only. We document the differences in household structure that exist across race and gender groups. We also consider associations between household structure, personal characteristics (such as maternal education), and family income. We then present results from estimated reduced-form equations in which the outcomes are estimated as functions of the household structure of young people at age 12.

These estimates are provided for the entire sample, separately for blacks, and further separately for black males and black females. The equations for the entire sample are used to estimate the extent to which differences in household structure across race and gender groups can account for differences in employment, educational, and behavioral outcomes across these groups. The separate equations for blacks and for black males and females enable us to estimate how household structure might affect outcomes differently within these groups, and how it might help account for group-specific trends over time.[18] In all three cases, we also estimate equations without and with controls for family income, to see the extent to which estimated impacts of household structure might work through family income. Finally, we present some estimates from individual and sibling fixed-effects models, to explore the extent to which our estimates are truly causal.

In Chapter 4, we analyze correlations between household structure and a number of other household characteristics, such as the following three:

1) Parenting style (e.g., whether parents are strict or supportive, how closely they monitor their children and are involved with them, and how structured family activities are),

2) The richness of the home environment, including the presence of computers or dictionaries and participation in various extra-curricular activities,

3) The quality of the neighborhood, as measured either by the survey respondent or by the surveyor.

We estimate reduced-form equations for employment, educational, and behavioral outcomes as functions of household structure as well as of these additional variables, to infer the extent to which the latter can help either to account for estimated effects of the former or to reinforce or offset these effects. These are also estimated for the sample as a whole and separately by race and gender.

In Chapter 5, we review our findings and consider their implications for policy and for further research.

OUR BASIC FINDINGS

The analyses in subsequent chapters find the following:

- Most young adults show positive trends in educational attainment and employment over time, but a gap remains between young blacks and Hispanics on the one hand and young whites on the other for both sets of outcomes. Young blacks also have children while unmarried and become incarcerated much more frequently than white or Hispanic youth. Within each racial group, progress has been greater for women than for men, and postsecondary school enrollments are now greater for women than for men in each racial group. Young black men, in particular, show the least improvement in almost all outcomes. Among black high school dropouts, the low rates of employment activity and high engagement in crime and other risky behaviors are pronounced.

- About half of young people today grow up in households without both biological parents, while about 80 percent of young blacks do so. Growing up without both biological parents appears to have modestly negative impacts on employment outcomes of young adults and more pronounced negative impacts on educational attainment, unmarried parenthood, and incarceration. The greater incidence of living with a single mother among blacks accounts for substantial portions of the racial differences among young adults in some outcomes, especially educational attainment, and also helps to account for a relative lack of progress (or even some deterioration) over time in these outcomes. The employment and incarceration outcomes of young black men are particularly strongly affected by growing up with a single mother. The lower family incomes of single-parent families—especially those headed by never-married mothers—account for some but not all of these impacts. And there is some evidence (from fixed-effects models) that these estimated negative effects of growing up with a single parent are at least partly causal.

- The negative effects of growing up in families without both parents are often compounded by the fact that these households tend to provide less enrichment to children and frequently are located in dangerous neighborhoods. Parenting behaviors are also related to household structure. Some of the parenting behaviors are likely caused, at least to some extent, by single parenthood. However, the human capital and neighborhood variables are more likely to be additional determinants of outcomes that happen to be correlated with structure, though the low family incomes and instability to which single parenthood contributes probably reinforce the observed gaps in these variables. Either way, these three sets of additional variables have jointly significant effects on most of the observed youth outcomes and can account for some substantial parts of the observed effects of household structure on these outcomes.

In short, youth and especially young minorities who grow up in single-parent families face a range of difficulties and disadvantages in terms of achieving academic or labor market success and staying out of trouble. Some of these difficulties appear to be caused by the singleness of their parents and some not. But in any case, they are truly swimming against the tide as they mature into young adulthood and beyond, in that they have less opportunity to succeed than their counterparts because of a variety of disadvantages that they experience.

At the same time, our findings illuminate a variety of personal and family characteristics that might be used to offset disadvantages and promote positive outcomes for young people, especially those in low-income and single-parent families. Sensible policies might seek to promote a variety of circumstances, including healthy marriages, more positive noncustodial fatherhood, higher incomes for working single parents, better schooling or employment options and safer neighborhoods for poor youth, and better child care and parenting among single parents. All of these would promote opportunity and success among otherwise disadvantaged youth. These broad approaches are explored in the book's concluding chapter.

Notes

1. The relative wages of less-educated young men were also declining during much of this period, implying that reduced work incentives were at least part of the reason for their diminishing work effort (Juhn 1992). Decreasing availability of blue-collar and manufacturing jobs, rising skill demands, rising competition from immigrants and women, "spatial mismatch" problems, and persistent discrimination have also likely contributed to the difficulties of young black men (Holzer 2000).

2. Ethnographic work suggests that employers perceive a stronger work ethic among Hispanics, especially immigrants; while they perceive more negative attitudes among young blacks and especially males (Wilson 1996). Fear of crime and violence, especially from those with criminal records, also appears to contribute to the problem. There is some evidence that employers who do not conduct formal criminal background checks engage in broad statistical discrimination against young black men as they seek to avoid hiring exoffenders (Holzer, Offner, and Sorensen 2005).

3. Johnson and Neal (1998) show that most of the black-white wage gap, but much less of the employment gap, disappears after controlling for racial differences in years of education and test scores. This evidence has been disputed by some authors (e.g., Rodgers and Spriggs 1996).

4. Educational attainment as measured in the Current Population Survey (CPS) does not carefully distinguish between GEDs and regular high school diplomas. For evidence on the weaker value of GEDs in the labor market, see Cameron and Heckman (1993).

5. See Ellwood and Jencks (2004) for a discussion about similarities and differences in trends in marriage and childbearing between more- and less-educated women over time. See also Edin and Kefalas (2005) for ethnographic evidence on the importance of marriage for low-income young women, despite their feeling that stable marriages might be unattainable, especially given the employment difficulties and unproductive behaviors that they perceive among the young men in their lives.

6. A number of authors (e.g., Graefe and Lichter 1999; Manning, Smock, and Majumdar 2004; Wu and Wolfe. 2001) have noted a growing trend towards cohabitation among unmarried parents in the United States, and that such unions tend to be shorter and more unstable than traditional marriages. But the effects of different patterns of cohabitation on youth outcomes, among both whites and minorities, have only recently been explored (Acs and Nelson 2003; Brown 2002; Dunifon and Kowaleski-Jones 2002; Manning and Lamb 2003).

7. Ashcraft and Lang (2006) discuss this literature and the potential upward and downward biases in various estimates of these effects.

8. Korenman and his colleagues conduct a variety of tests, including a comparison of siblings and cousins among children who were and were not born to single parents, the addition of controls for whether the pregnancy was intended or mistimed,

and instrumental variables (IVs) for the availability of abortion services and child support enforcement at the state level, as exogenous predictors of unwed births.

9. See also Stevenson and Wolfers (2007).

10. See also Stevenson and Wolfers (2007) for a more skeptical view of the causal effects of marriage and household structure on these outcomes.

11. Sigle-Rushton and McLanahan (2004) review these studies and the very mixed nature of their findings. Ashcraft and Lang (2006) discuss various reasons these studies might generate downward biases in estimates of negative effects associated with teen or unmarried childbearing.

12. See Mincy (1994) for a set of papers that focus on young black males in fatherless families. Lee et al. (1994) find stronger effects of absent mothers on their daughters but less evidence of stronger effects of absent fathers on sons.

13. In related literature, Garfinkel et al. (1998) looks at the role of child support payments by noncustodial fathers, and Holzer, Offner, and Sorensen (2005) examine the effects of child support enforcement on employment of young black men.

14. Similarly, Carneiro and Heckman (2003) note the importance of both cognitive and noncognitive "skills" on employment outcomes.

15. Hotz and Scholz (2001) describe reports that compare administrative and survey data reports on employment and income (especially for low-income populations); Kornfeld and Bloom (1999) examine the reliability (or lack of measurement error) of self-reported measures of earnings and employment; Abe (2001) and references therein discuss self-reports of antisocial behaviors, including comparisons across the NLSY79 and '97 cohorts, and differences by race and gender; and Laumann et al. (1994) discuss issues of reliability in survey questions about sexual behavior. The results of these studies are quite mixed but suggest that self-reported risky or illegal behaviors may be quite seriously underreported, relative to self-reported measures of employment or education.

16. A number of measures of family process and parenting style using such questions have been constructed by Child Trends (an independent, nonpartisan research center), under contract with the U.S. Department of Labor. These variables are available in the public use file as "family process" variables, and a separate data file appendix from Child Trends and the Center for Human Resource Research (1999) assesses the data quality, internal consistency and reliability, construct validity, and predictive validity.

17. We do not explore instrumental variable estimates because of our skepticism about the usefulness of some of these models, as noted earlier in the chapter.

18. Throughout our work in this monograph, we will use Chow tests to examine the statistical validity of pooling our estimates across race and gender groups as opposed to providing separate estimates for these groups.

2
Outcomes for Young
Adults in Two Cohorts

This chapter presents descriptive information about employment, education, and risky behaviors for young adults in the mid-1980s and the mid-2000s. In particular, we examine three areas: 1) employment outcomes of hourly wages, hours worked, and weeks worked; 2) educational outcomes of enrollment, degrees attained, high school test scores, and high school grade point averages (GPAs); and 3) engagement in risky behaviors of early substance use, childbearing while unmarried, and illegal activities. Simple descriptive statistics on these outcomes are presented for the full sample (separately by cohort) as well as by race and gender within each cohort. These statistics make it possible to examine differences across groups within a cohort, trends for a specific group across cohorts, and differences across groups across cohorts. Later in the chapter, we report descriptive statistics for additional outcomes for the more recent cohort of young adults and present regression estimates that show statistical relationships between their outcomes. The chapter concludes with a summary of the trends in young adults' outcomes over the past two decades.

SAMPLE

Our analysis in this chapter uses data from the 1979 and 1997 cohorts of the National Longitudinal Survey of Youth (NLSY79 and NLSY97). As we noted in Chapter 1, the NLSY79 is a nationally representative survey of more than 12,000 youth ages 14 to 21 as of December 31, 1978; and the NLSY97 is a nationally representative survey of almost 9,000 youth ages 12 to 16 as of December 31, 1996. The NLSY79 cohort was surveyed annually until 1994 and biannually afterwards. The NLSY97 cohort has been surveyed annually since 1997.

For descriptive analyses in the first part of this chapter, we impose three sample restrictions. First, to examine young adults of the same ages across the two cohorts (in Tables 2.1, 2.2, and 2.4), we include only young adults who were ages 22 to 24 at the time they were interviewed in either 1987 (for the early [NLSY79] cohort) or 2004–2005 (Round 8 for the later [NLSY97] cohort). These were the youngest members of the NLSY79 cohort (born primarily between 1962 and 1964) and the oldest members of the NLSY97 cohort (born primarily between 1980 and 1982). While all of these sample members were 22 to 24 at the time they were interviewed, the NLSY79 sample members were slightly older because the 1987 interviews were conducted mostly between April and June, while the 2004–2005 interviews were conducted mostly between November and January.[1]

We focus on the 1987 and 2004–2005 interviews because the 12 months prior to these dates represent similar points in the business cycle. While unemployment rates in late 1986–early 1987 were higher than those in 2004 (about 7.1 versus 5.5 percent), labor market tightness is comparable across the two years relative to most estimates of "full employment" for those periods.[2] The labor market was recovering from a steep recession in the former period and from a more modest downturn in the latter one.

For the second sample restriction, we include only the largest racial/ethnic subgroups: white non-Hispanics, black non-Hispanics, and Hispanics. For the third sample restriction (a relatively minor one) we exclude any persons who were still enrolled in high school and persons who were enrolled in college for whom the type (two-year or four-year) could not be reliably determined.[3] Regression analyses presented in the last part of the chapter (as well as sample means in Tables 2.3 and 2.5) are based on samples that include all ages of white, black, and Hispanic sample members from the NLSY97 only.

Another notable characteristic of the sample used in the analyses is that we include sample members who were incarcerated at the time of the survey.[4] Incarcerated individuals account for about 2 percent ($n = 69$) of our 22- to 24-year-old NLSY79 sample and 1.3 percent ($n = 51$) of our NLSY97 sample, but nearly 6.5 percent ($n = 29$) of young black men in the 1979 cohort and 6.2 percent ($n = 33$) of young black men in the 1997 cohort. The Bureau of Justice Statistics reports that roughly 12 percent of young black men between the ages of 16 and 34 are now incarcerated at any one time, while about twice that number are on parole or probation (Bureau of Justice Statistics 2007). Other analyses of this population that do not include incarcerated individuals contribute to the well-known undercount of young black men in census surveys (see, for example, Bound 1986 and Stark 1999). Of course, labor market outcomes of incarcerated individuals are predetermined, and including these observations in an analysis may result in findings that are unrepresentative of those who truly have choices to make. Thus, in addition to the estimates presented here, a full set of estimates that do not include incarcerated individuals is available from the authors on request. While the magnitudes of some results change, virtually no qualitative result is changed by the inclusion or omission of incarcerated individuals from the sample.

OUTCOME MEASURES

This chapter examines three categories of outcomes for young adults: employment, education, and risky behaviors.

For employment outcomes, we examine hourly wages, hours worked, and weeks worked. Wages are measured at the time of the survey or in the most recent job prior to the survey date.[5] To achieve comparability across the two NLSY cohorts, the wage rate includes tips and bonuses as well as regular wages. We adjust nominal wages for inflation to 2005 dollars using the Consumer Price Index Research Series Using Current Methods (CPI-U-RS), which is the Bureau of Labor Statistics' most complete effort to measure inflation and eliminate upward biases in the Consumer Price Index over time.[6] Hours and weeks worked are measured for the 52 weeks prior to the week of the interview.

For educational outcomes, we examine enrollment and educational attainment. We measure these variables in November for each cohort (1986 for the NLSY79 and 2004 for the NLSY97).[7] First, we classify each respondent as either not enrolled or enrolled. If not enrolled, we further classify the respondent by attainment: high school dropout or GED,[8] high school diploma, some college or associate's degree, or bachelor's degree or higher. If enrolled, we further classify the respondent by type of school: two-year college (including vocational and technical school) or four-year college or university (including graduate school).[9] For the 1997 cohort, we also examine educational outcomes of GPAs from high school transcripts as well as results from the Armed Services Vocational Aptitude Battery (ASVAB) tests.[10]

For risky behaviors and outcomes we examine measures from each cohort of whether the sample member drank alcohol, smoked cigarettes, or smoked marijuana before age 18; and whether she or he had a child and was unmarried as of the survey date in 1987 or 2004–2005.[11] For the 1997 cohort only, we examine whether the sample member had ever engaged in illegal activities, been arrested, or been incarcerated.[12]

The variables for drinking alcohol, smoking cigarettes, and smoking marijuana before age 18 were all created in a similar way in both the NLSY79 and NLSY97: With information about the sample member's birth date, as well as self-reported information about the date at which the respondent first drank alcohol (or smoked a cigarette or marijuana), we created binary variables indicating whether the sample member had engaged in each activity before his or her eighteenth birthday.

To measure whether the sample member was unmarried with a child by the time of the interview in 1987 or 2004–2005, we used information from the fertility and relationship history taken in the 1987 round of the NLSY79, and information about birth dates of sample members' children in the NLSY97.

Engaging in illegal activity is measured with a series of self-reported responses indicating whether the sample member in the NLSY97 had ever been engaged (prior to the latest survey date) in relatively less serious or less violent activity (for example, had ever damaged property or stolen something worth more than $50), as well as relatively more serious or more violent activity (for example, had ever attacked someone, carried a handgun, or been arrested). We also measure whether the sample member had ever been incarcerated, using information on the place of residence at the time of the survey in each year as well as self-reports of incarceration. The tendency for self-reported crime and incarceration rates to understate actual rates may be substantial, particularly for minorities (Hindelang, Hirschi, and Weis 1981). For this reason, we have constructed an incarceration rate based at least partly on information that is independent of potentially biased self-reported information.

LIMITATIONS

This chapter's findings are characterized by limitations arising from the time at which we observe young adults in the two cohorts, and from their self-reports of risky behaviors and crime. First, the periods during which we observe the two NLSY cohorts are not ideal for the purpose of comparing behaviors and outcomes across time. As noted, to compare young adults of the same ages at similar points in a business cycle, we examine outcomes in 1986–1987 and 2004–2005. Yet real wages of less-educated workers stagnated or declined over the period 1973–1995, then rose thereafter. Thus, the time frame we examine combines a period of modestly declining real wages with a period of significantly rising real wages, masking the actual trend in earnings. Another timing issue, noted earlier, is that interviews were conducted primarily from April to June in 1987 and from November to January in 2004–2005. Ideally, these survey months would be identical (or more similar) across the survey cohorts and years.

Sample members' self-reports of risky and criminal behaviors constitute a second limitation of the analyses. Self-reports, especially of risky behaviors or crime, may be underreported because of the stigma associated with these actions. Self-reports of criminal activity may be differentially underreported among blacks (Abe 2001; Hindelang, Hirschi, and Weis 1981; Viscusi 1986). It may be, however, that the stigma associated with these behaviors has fallen over time; we are not aware of more recent research investigating this issue. Furthermore, the dichotomous measure we use (whether the sample member engaged in a particular activity) is a less precise measure of the activity than a frequency measure would be. All in all, these measurement issues likely bias the estimated relationships in our regressions towards zero or insignificant results.[13] Our measure of incarceration, however, is less likely to suffer from measurement error because it is based on both self-reports and place of residence at the time of the survey.

In part because of these limitations, our regression estimates should not be interpreted as showing causal effects. However, as most of the biases noted above should not be more severe in one cohort or another or in any particular race or gender group, these biases should not affect the inferences we draw regarding trends over time and differences across these groups.

EMPIRICAL FINDINGS

We first present descriptive statistics for employment and educational outcomes, then for risky behaviors, for young adults ages 22–24 in 1986–1987 and in 2004–2005. Next, focusing on the more recent cohort, we present results from regression analyses predicting wages, weeks worked, and high school dropout status.[14]

Descriptive Statistics on Employment Outcomes

Table 2.1 presents descriptive statistics for employment outcomes of hourly wages, hours worked, and weeks worked. These outcomes are presented separately by cohort for the 22- to 24-year-old subsample, and separately by race and gender within each cohort. In general, Table 2.1 shows (consistent with other studies) that males tend to earn more, and work more hours and weeks, than do females; and that hourly wages for blacks tend to be lower than for whites, as do hours and weeks worked (where the difference is relatively larger).

With regard to trends across the cohorts, overall the results in Table 2.1 indicate that real wages and weeks worked each have grown about 7 percent.[15] The greatest gains in hours and weeks worked of any group were experienced by black and Hispanic females. This growth has been widely attributed to policy changes in the 1990s, primarily welfare reform and expansion of supports for low-income working parents such as the Earned Income Tax Credit (EITC) and child care benefits (Blank 2002). In contrast, hours worked fell the most for white and black men (though only the results for the latter are statistically significant). The results for both groups are mostly driven by outcomes among the less educated, as noted by Juhn (1992, 2000).

Despite these trends, many of the race and gender gaps observed in the earlier cohort persist in the more recent one. Within each racial group, women still have lower wages, hours worked, and weeks worked than men,[16] though they exhibit greater improvement than men in al-

Table 2.1 Means of Employment Outcomes, by Gender and Race

	Hourly wages ($)		Total hours worked		Weeks worked	
	1987	2005	1987	2005	1987	2005
Full sample	11.40	12.21	1,490	1,469	36.2	38.9
By gender and race						
Male						
White	12.65	12.97	1,672	1,613	38.1	41.3
Black	10.41	11.20	1,419	1,262	33.3	34.0
Hispanic	11.66	13.80	1,574	1,644	37.6	41.4
Female						
White	10.78	11.89	1,402	1,419	36.5	39.2
Black	8.93	10.39	1,121	1,223	29.0	33.1
Hispanic	9.90	11.20	1,151	1,307	29.7	35.1
Sample size	2,713	3,186	3,289	4,164	3,333	4,164

NOTE: Samples include respondents ages 22–24 at the time of interview. Hourly wages are in 2005 dollars, deflated by the CPI-U-RS and measured for the current or most recent job at the time of interview. 1987 NLSY79 interviews occurred between March 1987 and October 1987 and Round 8 NLSY97 interviews occurred between October 2004 and July 2005. Hours and weeks worked are measured for the 52 weeks prior to the week of interview.
SOURCE: Authors' tabulations from NLSY79 and NLSY97.

most all cases. These trends are consistent with prior research showing that female labor force activity has grown more rapidly than that of males for several decades (Juhn and Potter 2006) and in the 1980s corresponded with more rapid wage growth (Blau and Kahn 1997).

With regard to race gaps within gender, these data indicate that Hispanics have achieved greater parity with whites in labor market outcomes in the later cohort than had been observed earlier, despite strong immigration growth over this time period.[17] But black men have fallen even further behind young white and Hispanic men in terms of hours and weeks worked, a finding that remains even when incarcerated individuals are removed from the sample.[18] Some gain in relative wages for black men compared to white men is observed: the gap between the wages of white and black men shrank from 18 percent in 1987 to 14 percent in 2005. However, this pattern is likely driven by the withdrawal of lower-wage workers from the labor force altogether (Chandra 2003), and thus is an artifact of the composition of the wage-earning sample.

The relative decline in employment for young black men over the 1980s and 1990s, and the sharp contrast between their employment trends and those of young black women, has been noted elsewhere (Holzer and Offner 2006), based on data from the Current Population Survey (CPS). This similarity between the CPS data and the NLSY data is notable because self-reported employment information (such as that obtained in the NLSY79 and NLSY97) may be more accurate for young adults than that reported by household respondents on the CPS (e.g., Freeman and Medoff 1982).

Descriptive Statistics on Education Outcomes

Table 2.2 shows information on school enrollment and educational attainment for the two cohorts, once again reported separately by race and gender within cohort. These data indicate that the high school dropout rate has declined overall and for most race and gender groups, though controversy remains over the trends in high school dropout rates, driven by differences observed between survey data such as these and school administrative data (Mishel and Roy 2006; Swanson 2004).

Widespread increases in college enrollment and educational attainment are observed among young adults across these two cohorts. Enrollment in two-year colleges has more than doubled for every race and gender group, though enrollment in four-year colleges and universities remains greater for each group. Bachelor's degree attainment has grown modestly. Turner (2007) and others have noted a widening gap between college attendance and completion, as well as a tendency for those who attain four-year degrees to take longer to do so. Indeed, the fact that more young people in the 22–24 age range are now enrolled in four-year colleges than have already graduated with bachelor's degrees reflects the longer time period now taken to complete these degrees, whether for reasons of financial need and constraints or because of personal tastes.[19] Nonetheless, these data indicate some significant educational improvements for young people over the past two decades.

But, as in the case of employment outcomes, some gaps remain across groups in school enrollment and educational attainment. In particular, blacks and Hispanics continue to drop out of high school more frequently than whites, and less frequently attend or graduate from four-year colleges. Orfield (2004) discusses the dropout issue in de-

Table 2.2 Educational Attainment and Enrollment Status, by Gender and Race (%)

| | Not enrolled | | | | | | | | Enrolled | | | | | |
| | High school dropout/GED | | High school diploma | | Some college/ associate's degree | | Bachelor's degree | | Two-year college | | Four-year college | | n | |
	1986	2004	1986	2004	1986	2004	1986	2004	1986	2004	1986	2004	1986	2004
Full sample	19.23	15.54	30.51	27.18	24.78	22.37	10.83	12.45	2.65	6.29	12.00	16.17	3,361	4,170
By gender and race														
Male														
White	19.53	13.37	29.23	30.36	21.50	21.21	11.38	12.81	2.68	5.07	15.68	17.17	958	1,039
Black	28.05	27.60	34.95	30.78	22.68	20.74	2.23	5.57	2.24	5.65	9.86	9.66	456	564
Hispanic	38.27	20.79	24.41	34.28	21.98	23.22	3.65	3.63	3.51	7.97	8.17	10.11	293	452
Female														
White	14.82	12.03	31.32	21.14	26.48	22.95	14.35	18.15	2.56	6.75	10.48	18.97	922	1,016
Black	19.11	19.00	33.49	28.39	33.89	23.58	4.60	6.89	3.12	7.75	5.79	14.40	425	611
Hispanic	28.09	20.55	26.75	27.60	33.15	25.38	2.40	5.52	2.30	7.73	7.31	13.21	307	488

NOTE: Sample includes all respondents ages 22–24 at the time of interview. Enrollment is measured in the month of November. The sum of each gender and race group's enrollment statuses for each cohort equals 100.

SOURCE: Authors' tabulations from NLSY79 and NLSY97.

tail. We examine the extent to which higher dropout rates among young minorities can be accounted for by achievement or family background differences later in this chapter and in Chapter 3.

Rates of improvement over time in enrollment and educational attainment also vary across groups. High school dropout rates have declined most dramatically for young Hispanics, while college enrollment and attainment have risen more among whites than among minorities. In general, educational attainment has risen more rapidly among young women than among young men within each racial group, especially whites.

The tendency to drop out of high school is higher for boys than for girls within each racial group in both cohorts, but four-year college enrollment and attainment of degrees are higher for women only in the more recent cohort. The growth of a gender gap in education favoring women has been noted elsewhere (Jacob 2002), and its seriousness has been debated recently (e.g., Mead 2006). But the magnitudes of the gender gaps in education among both whites and blacks are striking.

Furthermore, young black men have made less progress in completing high school and enrolling in four-year colleges than any other race or gender group. In particular, their tendency to drop out of high school has not changed, and now it is higher than that observed for any other group. Thus the trends in educational attainment among young black men parallel those observed earlier for employment, suggesting a broad pattern of relative decline in socioeconomic status.

Table 2.3 presents data on grade point averages and ASVAB percentile scores for the 1997 cohort by race and gender. High school GPAs and ASVAB percentile scores are lower, on average, for Hispanics and especially for blacks, compared with whites (see also Jencks and Phillips 1998). Within racial groups, young women have comparable or higher outcomes than young men, and relatively large gaps are observed between young black women and men. That gender differences in grades are somewhat larger than differences in ASVAB percentiles suggests behavioral, rather than cognitive, differences in school outcomes by gender.

The reasons for the persistence of the achievement gap between whites and minorities remain somewhat unclear in the broader literature (Neal 2005). Though the gap narrowed during the 1980s, it stabilized or even widened slightly afterwards (Hauser and Huang 1996). Racial

Table 2.3 Means on Education Outcomes, by Gender and Race

	High school GPA	ASVAB
Full sample	2.43	51.18
By gender and race		
Male		
White	2.47	57.34
Black	1.86	28.14
Hispanic	2.05	39.39
Female		
White	2.66	58.20
Black	2.18	32.01
Hispanic	2.34	38.76
Sample size	5,119	5,810

NOTE: Sample includes all youth in NLSY97 as of Round 8.
SOURCE: Authors' tabulations from NLSY97.

gaps in family income and the persistence of school segregation play some role (Card and Rothstein 2005), though they cannot fully explain the persistence of achievement gaps. Indeed, a racial gap in achievement is observed early (appearing before children start school), and having a young, single mother contributes to lower scores (Fryer and Levitt 2004). But whether differences in household structure, parental characteristics, and parenting behavior can account for much of the existing racial gap in achievement and its failure to close over time merits further study.

Descriptive Statistics on Risky Behaviors

The next set of tables presents information on the extent to which young people have engaged in various risky behaviors across the two cohorts, with additional measures reported for the more recent cohort. Table 2.4 presents data on use of substances—alcohol, cigarettes, and marijuana—prior to the sample member's eighteenth birthday, as well as data on having had a child while unmarried at any time before the survey date in 1987 or 2004–2005. As before, these results are presented for all youth and separately by race and gender within cohort.

Table 2.4 shows some decline in cigarette and marijuana smoking across the two cohorts, a trend reported elsewhere (Gruber 2001). In

Table 2.4 Risky Behaviors: Substance Use and Unmarried Childbearing, by Gender and Race (%)

	Drank alcohol		Smoked cigarettes		Smoked marijuana		Unmarried, has children	
	NLSY79	NLSY97	NLSY79	NLSY97	NLSY79	NLSY97	NLSY79	NLSY97
Full sample	74.2	73.8	74.2	60.7	48.0	40.7	12.6	19.0
By gender and race								
Male								
White	78.0	77.5	78.4	64.8	53.2	43.6	5.7	9.9
Black	77.9	56.6	67.4	49.2	47.1	40.4	27.1	30.8
Hispanic	82.8	74.1	73.6	56.5	56.4	39.9	15.3	17.9
Female								
White	71.0	79.7	75.6	66.3	47.3	42.9	10.6	17.3
Black	61.4	59.4	57.3	43.1	25.7	27.1	43.0	47.5
Hispanic	66.1	60.9	58.6	48.5	31.5	30.8	21.5	29.6
Sample size	2,968	4,191	3,317	4,188	3,341	4,177	3,361	4,180

NOTE: Sample includes respondents ages 22–24 at the time of the 1987 and Round 8 interviews. The 1987 NLSY79 interviews occurred between March 1987 and October 1987, and the Round 8 NLSY97 interviews occurred between October 2004 and July 2005. Substance-use variables measure use of substance by the respondent's eighteenth birthday.
SOURCE: Authors' tabulations from NLSY79 and NLSY97.

general, minorities and especially blacks self-report less drinking and smoking than do whites. Declines over time in self-reported substance use also appear greater among blacks than among others, at least for alcohol use and cigarette smoking.

In contrast, it is clear that unmarried childbearing has risen in frequency across the two cohorts for all groups and remains most pronounced among young blacks. The greater frequency of unmarried childbearing among young blacks reflects both low levels of marriage and greater declines in childbearing among black married women relative to other groups (Wu and Wolfe 2001). Among both whites and minorities but especially among African Americans, more-educated women appear to be delaying both marriage and childbearing, while less-educated women have decoupled the two behaviors, putting off childbearing less than they might if they expected higher marriage rates in the future (Edin and Kefalas 2005; Ellwood and Jencks 2004).

The dramatic differences in employment and educational trends between young black men and women noted above are also consistent with low marriage rates for them, as the men become less marriageable and the women become more independent (Tucker and Mitchell-Kernan 1995), and if childbearing fails to fall as rapidly as marriage, then we would expect the relative growth in out-of-wedlock childbearing for this group to be highest.

In the past decade, the rates of unmarried childbearing have largely stabilized for most groups, though they have not dramatically declined (McLanahan 2004). Also, Table 2.4 indicates that rates of reported childbearing outside of marriage are generally higher among young women than among young men, likely reflecting either a tendency of older men to father these children or a greater reluctance among men to report these outcomes.

Table 2.5 presents descriptive statistics on another important dimension of risky behavior among young adults, namely, whether they have ever participated in illegal activities or been incarcerated. Because information about these variables during the teen years is available only for the 1997 cohort, and because the sample no longer needs to be restricted to obtain a consistent range of ages appearing in both cohorts, the full sample of 19- to 25-year-olds from the NLSY97 (as of Round 8) is used. Statistics are presented for the full sample, then separately by race and gender. Self-reported outcomes that are given in the tables

36

Table 2.5 Means on Engagement in Risky Behaviors, by Gender and Race (%)

	Ever damaged property	Ever stole items worth more than $50	Ever joined a gang	Ever carried a handgun	Ever sold drugs	Ever attacked someone	Ever arrested	Ever incarcerated
Full sample	41.6	21.1	11.0	22.7	23.8	34.4	27.9	5.9
By gender and race								
Male								
White	55.3	27.9	11.3	35.7	29.7	40.1	34.9	7.6
Black	44.8	27.6	25.9	36.8	28.7	52.5	45.0	14.8
Hispanic	47.5	28.7	21.6	33.8	28.9	43.6	38.2	9.6
Female								
White	30.7	13.6	5.7	9.0	20.2	22.6	18.9	2.7
Black	30.1	15.7	8.5	8.5	9.7	38.6	19.1	3.1
Hispanic	26.0	13.4	9.8	10.4	15.6	26.6	15.2	2.4
Sample size	6,992	6,963	7,143	7,125	6,957	6,990	7,133	7,073

NOTE: Sample includes all NLSY97 sample members. Variables are measured up to Round 8 (conducted from October 2004 to July 2005).

SOURCE: Authors' tabulations from NLSY97.

concern whether the respondent reported ever engaging in less serious offenses (damaging property, stealing something valued at more than $50, or joining a gang) or more serious offenses (carrying a handgun, selling drugs, attacking someone, or being arrested). We also present a measure of ever having been incarcerated, based both on self-reports and on whether the interview ever took place while the respondent was incarcerated.

Table 2.5 shows relatively high rates of self-reported activity in minor offenses such as ever damaging property (with over 40 percent of young respondents and roughly half of young men reporting such activity) and somewhat lower activity in more serious crime categories. Over one-third of all young men report having ever carried a handgun or having ever been arrested. These rates seem quite high, though we know of no reason why these self-reported rates might be upwardly biased. Young women report much less such activity than young men in each category.

Self-reported illegal activity among young black men in many of these categories is lower than or comparable to that of white men, which might reflect a greater tendency towards underreporting of such activity. Yet in some categories (such as attacking someone or joining a gang), self-reported rates for young black men are higher.

Observed rates of incarceration among young black men are considerably higher than among young white men (14.8 percent versus 7.6 percent). Indeed, data from the Bureau of Justice Statistics (2007) show that incarceration rates of young black men are roughly six times as high as they are for young white men, and that nearly a third of all young black men have spent some time in prison by their early 30s. The statistics in Table 2.5 are based on a sample of 19- to 25-year-olds, so it is not surprising that the rates are somewhat lower than the BJS rates. On the other hand, the incarceration rate in Table 2.5 might be understated because self-reported incarceration will likely understate its frequency, and the use of interviews in prison to designate incarceration will miss short spells that occur between annual interviews.

Overall, these data clearly indicate high rates of unmarried childbirth among young blacks and very high rates of incarceration among young black men, relative to all other race and ethnic groups. These data are consistent with the relatively weak outcomes and trends over time for these men in education and especially in employment.[20]

REGRESSION ANALYSIS OF EMPLOYMENT AND EDUCATION OUTCOMES

Table 2.6 presents regressions predicting employment and educational outcomes for the full sample of NLSY97 youth, ranging from 19 to 25 years old. Overall, these results show some strong behavioral patterns: young people who fail at school also more frequently engage in risky behavior and withdraw from the labor market. Among blacks and black males especially these patterns are quite pronounced.

The following general models are estimated in this section:

(2.1) $LNWAGE_i, WW_i = f(X_i, ED_i, ACH_i, RISKBEH_i) + u_i$;

(2.2) $HSDROPOUT_i, = f(X_i, ACH_i, RISKBEH_i) + v_i$,

where $LNWAGE$ represents the natural log of hourly wage, WW represents weeks worked in the previous year, and $HSDROPOUT$ represents whether or not the respondent dropped out of high school or obtained a GED ($HSDROPOUT = 1$ if dropout or GED; 0 if not dropout or GED). A set of exogenous personal characteristics is represented by X, which includes personal demographic characteristics such as race, gender, and age. ED represents a series of indicator variables for enrollment status and attainment; ACH represents cognitive achievement in high school, measured by ASVAB percentile scores and high school GPA; $RISKBEH$ represents engagement in any of the set of risky behaviors (including incarceration) defined above; and the subscript i denotes the ith individual.[21]

In this formulation, as shown in Equations (2.1) and (2.2), both labor market outcomes and educational attainment are functions of demographic characteristics, cognitive achievement, and engaging in risky behaviors. As shown in Equation (2.1), labor market outcomes also depend on educational enrollment status and attainment, as well as on the other variables independent of education. As such, the models described here are recursive in nature. Of course, engaging in risky behaviors is not likely to be strictly exogenous with respect to these outcomes; these relationships should be viewed as partial correlations that represent patterns of behaviors and outcomes across different groups of young people.

All equations are estimated using Ordinary Least Squares (OLS); thus, the equations for dropping out of high school are linear probability models. The goal is to estimate race and gender differences in outcomes (controlling only for age) without and then with adjustments for differences in educational attainment, cognitive achievement, and engaging in risky behaviors. In particular, for each outcome, three specifications are presented. Model 1 includes only the X variables; Model 2 adds educational attainment and cognitive achievement (with only the latter added to the equation for dropping out of high school); and Model 3 adds the indicators for risky behaviors.

The results of Model 1 in Table 2.6 mostly confirm a set of differences in outcomes by race and gender that were observed earlier in the simple descriptive statistics, though the point estimates differ because of the broadening of the sample to include all NLSY97 sample members.[22] For instance, the wages of black males are 11 percent lower than those of white males ($e^{-0.116} - 1$) and wages of black females 18 percent lower than those of white males. Weeks worked among blacks and Hispanic females are also lower than those of white males, with the largest negative effects (about eight weeks fewer on average) occurring among black males. Dropping out of high school is most common among blacks and Hispanics: black male and Hispanic male dropout rates are 13 and 11 percentage points higher than those of white males. In this sample, white females have wages lower than (or statistically comparable to) those of black and Hispanic women.

The results of Model 2 show that educational attainment and achievement are importantly related to labor market outcomes. High school dropouts and graduates (as well as those enrolled in four-year colleges) have lower wages and weeks worked than college graduates. Test scores contribute to both sets of outcomes independently of educational attainment.

The magnitudes of the effects of education and achievement vary across labor market outcomes. For instance, their effect on wages is large: college graduates earn about 26 percent higher wages than high school dropouts, controlling for achievement. The latter measures add modestly to these differences, with each point of GPA adding about 1 percent to wages (though the effect is not statistically significant), and

Table 2.6 Recursive Regressions Predicting Employment and Education Outcomes

	Natural log of hourly wage, past year			Weeks worked, past year			High school dropout, Nov. 2004		
	Model 1	Model 2	Model 3	Model 1	Model 2	Model 3	Model 1	Model 2	Model 3
Race (omitted category: white male)									
Black male	-0.116***	-0.083***	-0.073***	-8.200***	-5.663***	-4.755***	0.134***	-0.026	-0.032**
	(0.019)	(0.020)	(0.020)	(0.811)	(0.805)	(0.809)	(0.018)	(0.017)	(0.016)
Hispanic male	0.021	0.050**	0.050**	-0.356	1.339*	1.522*	0.106***	-0.004	0.004
	(0.020)	(0.020)	(0.021)	(0.790)	(0.793)	(0.792)	(0.019)	(0.017)	(0.016)
White female	-0.161***	-0.172***	-0.179***	-2.015***	-2.172***	-2.500***	-0.018	0.013	0.023**
	(0.017)	(0.017)	(0.018)	(0.590)	(0.587)	(0.601)	(0.012)	(0.011)	(0.010)
Black female	-0.196***	-0.172***	-0.170***	-7.763***	-6.216***	-5.433***	0.048***	-0.052***	-0.042***
	(0.019)	(0.019)	(0.020)	(0.770)	(0.768)	(0.798)	(0.016)	(0.014)	(0.014)
Hispanic female	-0.121***	-0.100***	-0.106***	-5.993***	-4.704***	-4.740***	0.057***	-0.027*	-0.001
	(0.020)	(0.021)	(0.021)	(0.821)	(0.820)	(0.828)	(0.018)	(0.016)	(0.016)
Age	0.068***	0.053***	0.054***	1.457***	1.046***	1.163***	-0.005	-0.002	-0.008***
	(0.004)	(0.004)	(0.004)	(0.155)	(0.161)	(0.162)	(0.003)	(0.003)	(0.003)
Education level (omitted category: not enrolled, bachelor's degree)									
Not enrolled, high school dropout or GED		-0.297***	-0.267***		-9.047***	-6.779***			
		(0.032)	(0.033)		(1.082)	(1.125)			
Not enrolled, high school diploma		-0.220***	-0.207***		-0.478	0.511			
		(0.029)	(0.029)		(0.912)	(0.926)			

Not enrolled, some college or associate's degree	-0.201*** (0.029)	-0.191*** (0.029)	0.869 (0.874)	1.608* (0.882)		
Enrolled, two-year college	-0.256*** (0.032)	-0.247*** (0.033)	0.109 (1.101)	0.761 (1.109)		
Enrolled, four-year college	-0.294*** (0.029)	-0.291*** (0.029)	-5.942*** (0.904)	-5.683*** (0.907)		
GPA in high school	0.011 (0.012)	0.008 (0.012)	0.922** (0.450)	0.808* (0.454)	-0.184*** (0.009)	-0.141*** (0.009)
ASVAB percentile	0.026*** (0.008)	0.026*** (0.008)	1.504*** (0.311)	1.359*** (0.311)	-0.073*** (0.006)	-0.056*** (0.005)
Unmarried and has children	-0.024 (0.015)		-3.109*** (0.624)			0.123*** (0.013)
Risky behaviors prior to age 18						
Drank alcohol	0.034** (0.014)		1.146* (0.587)			-0.026*** (0.010)
Smoked cigarettes	0.007 (0.014)		1.188** (0.551)			0.044*** (0.010)
Smoked marijuana	-0.023 (0.014)		0.016 (0.553)			0.026** (0.010)
Ever stole something worth $50 or more, joined a gang, attacked someone, or was arrested	-0.027** (0.013)		-1.602*** (0.520)			0.054*** (0.009)

(continued)

Table 2.6 (continued)

	Natural log of hourly wage, past year			Weeks worked, past year			High school dropout, Nov. 2004		
	Model 1	Model 2	Model 3	Model 1	Model 2	Model 3	Model 1	Model 2	Model 3
Ever incarcerated			-0.049*			-5.117***			0.265***
			(0.027)			(1.055)			(0.023)
Constant	0.548	1.042**	1.031**	9.229	21.582***	20.880**	0.390***	0.672***	0.556***
	(0.341)	(0.419)	(0.442)	(7.624)	(8.014)	(8.174)	(0.086)	(0.082)	(0.078)
Observations	5,849	5,849	5,849	7,085	7,085	7,085	7,115	7,115	7,115
R-squared	0.077	0.108	0.112	0.041	0.097	0.108	0.028	0.217	0.284

NOTE: Robust standard errors are shown in parentheses. Variables are measured in Round 8 of the NLSY97, from October 2004 to July 2005. Dummy variables controlling for month of interview are included but not reported. Missing data dummies are included for all explanatory variables except for race/gender. Statistical significance is denoted as follows: * $p < 0.10$; ** $p < 0.05$; *** $p < 0.01$.
SOURCE: Authors' tabulations from NLSY97.

test score differences between the very best and worst scores adding about 3 percent to the wages of those with the best scores. These wage differences may widen as these young people age and their differences in ability and job performance become more observable to employers and affect wage growth over time (Altonji and Pierret 2001).

The negative effect of being a high school dropout on weeks worked is quite strong, with dropouts working almost nine weeks less on average than nonenrolled high school and college graduates (relative to overall sample means of about 39 weeks worked per year). Achievement differences between the best and worst students would add to these effects by a few additional weeks.

The results of Table 2.6 also show that differences in education and test scores account for only modest parts of the differences observed in labor market outcomes across racial groups in the NLSY97 data. Among men, education and achievement can account for about a third of wage and weeks-worked differences by race; among women, they account for less than a third of observed differences in weeks worked. These results are contrary to prior studies using the NLSY79 (e.g., Johnson and Neal 1998), and this finding may not hold as this more recent cohort ages (recall that sample members are only 19 to 25 years old at this point).[23] The finding implies that scholastic achievement is only one of several important mechanisms through which young blacks are disadvantaged in the labor market.

But Table 2.6 also shows that achievement differences fully account for racial differences in the tendency to drop out of high school. In other words, when they have similar levels of school achievement, blacks tend to drop out of high school less than whites, and Hispanics drop out at similar rates. Prior research has noted a similar pattern (e.g., Lang and Manove 2006), suggesting the potential influence of achievement equalization on employment outcomes.

Finally, in Model 3, including indicators for risky behaviors adds modest explanatory power, especially in predicting high school dropout rates. Relatively few of these risky behavior measures—except for incarceration—are related to wages while controlling for education and achievement. But being an unmarried parent is associated with reduced weeks worked, as is participation in illegal activities, getting arrested, and especially being incarcerated.[24] Whether these incarceration effects are causal or merely reflect the self-selection of weak labor market participants into illegal activity cannot be ascertained here, though other studies suggest that the incarceration effects are at least partly causal (Holzer, Offner, and Sorensen 2005; Raphael 2007; Western 2006). By definition, those who are currently incarcerated cannot work, but even when the currently incarcerated are removed from the sample, weeks-worked effects remain for those ever incarcerated.[25]

Several of the measures added in Model 3, particularly unmarried childbearing and incarceration, are positively and strongly associated with the tendency to drop out of high school—for instance, dropout rates that are 12 percentage points higher for unmarried parents and 27 percentage points higher for those who have ever been incarcerated. Controlling for incarceration, higher dropout rates can be found among those engaging in serious crime and even among those smoking cigarettes or marijuana before age 18. This indicates that engaging in such behaviors increases the probability of failing in and disconnecting from the world of school.

Table 2.7 shows the same set of estimated equations, limiting the sample to blacks only. (Tables A.1 and A.2, found in Appendix A, show separate regressions for black males and black females.)[26] The overall patterns for blacks are similar to those for the full sample: education and achievement are associated with labor market outcomes, and risky behaviors are somewhat correlated with the tendency to drop out of high school.

Yet many of the statistical relationships are stronger among young blacks and especially black females than in the overall sample. For example, the effects of education and achievement on wages are generally higher for blacks (especially black females) than for other groups. The negative effect of being a high school dropout on weeks worked is stronger for blacks than for whites and Hispanics; and the relationships between incarceration, on the one hand, and low work effort or dropping out, on the other, are very strong among young blacks. The effects of achievement on labor market outcomes and dropping out of high school are also quite strong for blacks and especially black males.

CONCLUSION

This chapter describes broad trends across two cohorts in the education and employment of young adults and in race and gender differences in these outcomes. Key findings from this chapter include the following:

- Employment outcomes have, on average, remained fairly constant or improved a bit among young adults, while educational outcomes have improved more substantially between the mid- to late 1980s and the mid-2000s.

- Traditional gender gaps in employment outcomes are diminishing, and a new educational gap favoring young women over men is becoming pronounced in each racial group.

- Employment and educational outcomes are lower for blacks compared with whites. Young black men generally show less progress (or more deterioration) in these areas than other groups, including young black women.

- Those who drop out of high school have much lower academic achievement and are also most likely to engage in risky behaviors (such as having children outside of marriage and participating in crime) and to not work, especially among young blacks.

In the subsequent chapters, we examine the extent to which these outcomes—especially the patterns by race—can be attributed to household structure and parental characteristics and behaviors. For now, we note the wide gaps in successful educational and employment outcomes between young blacks and other groups, especially for young black men and especially for those who fail to complete high school.

Table 2.7 Recursive Regressions Predicting Employment and Education Outcomes for Black Males and Females

	Natural log of hourly wage, past year			Weeks worked, past year			High school dropout, Nov. 2004		
	Model 1	Model 2	Model 3	Model 1	Model 2	Model 3	Model 1	Model 2	Model 3
Gender (omitted category: male)									
Female	−0.083***	−0.087***	−0.090***	1.460	−0.063	−0.924	−0.081***	−0.007	0.018
	(0.020)	(0.020)	(0.022)	(0.914)	(0.905)	(0.959)	(0.020)	(0.018)	(0.018)
Age	0.059***	0.051***	0.052***	1.580***	1.184***	1.243***	−0.007	−0.005	−0.010*
	(0.007)	(0.008)	(0.008)	(0.316)	(0.322)	(0.326)	(0.007)	(0.006)	(0.006)
Education level (omitted category: not enrolled, bachelor's degree)									
Not enrolled, high school dropout or GED		−0.278***	−0.258***		−14.559***	−12.364***			
		(0.055)	(0.057)		(2.145)	(2.223)			
Not enrolled, high school diploma		−0.186***	−0.179***		−7.566***	−6.794***			
		(0.051)	(0.052)		(1.861)	(1.883)			
Not enrolled, some college or associate's degree		−0.147***	−0.139***		−3.460*	−2.803			
		(0.050)	(0.052)		(1.779)	(1.809)			
Enrolled, two-year college		−0.230***	−0.222***		−6.722***	−5.930***			
		(0.059)	(0.060)		(2.210)	(2.254)			
Enrolled, four-year college		−0.221***	−0.220***		−7.541***	−7.209***			
		(0.056)	(0.057)		(1.936)	(1.936)			
GPA in high school		−0.048**	−0.049**		1.304	1.023		−0.198***	−0.157***
		(0.021)	(0.022)		(0.871)	(0.877)		(0.016)	(0.016)
ASVAB percentile		0.080***	0.079***		1.949***	2.060***		−0.101***	−0.086***
		(0.015)	(0.015)		(0.683)	(0.691)		(0.012)	(0.012)

47

	(1)	(2)	(3)	(4)	(5)	(6)	(7)	(8)	(9)
Unmarried and has children			−0.017			−0.025			0.077***
			(0.023)			(1.014)			(0.019)
Risky behaviors prior to age 18									
Drank alcohol			0.003			−1.282			−0.034*
			(0.023)			(1.036)			(0.018)
Smoked cigarettes			−0.014			0.718			0.096***
			(0.022)			(1.049)			(0.019)
Smoked marijuana			0.005			−0.452			0.048**
			(0.024)			(1.139)			(0.021)
Ever stole something worth $50 or more, joined a gang, attacked someone, or was arrested			0.009			−1.909*			0.051***
			(0.022)			(1.014)			(0.017)
Ever incarcerated			−0.058			−6.603***			0.250***
			(0.041)			(1.875)			(0.038)
Constant	0.880***	1.410***	1.374***	−14.761*	5.681	9.186	0.720***	0.806***	0.622***
	(0.188)	(0.225)	(0.228)	(8.181)	(8.968)	(9.087)	(0.174)	(0.158)	(0.150)
Observations	1,493	1,493	1,493	1,941	1,941	1,941	1,964	1,964	1,964
R-squared	0.064	0.113	0.118	0.023	0.098	0.113	0.028	0.250	0.321

NOTE: Robust standard errors are shown in parentheses. Variables are measured in Round 8 of the NLSY97, from October 2004 to July 2005. Dummy variables controlling for month of interview are included but not reported. Missing data dummies are included for all explanatory variables except for race/gender. Statistical significance is denoted as follows: * $p < 0.10$; ** $p < 0.05$; *** $p < 0.01$.
SOURCE: Authors' tabulations from NLSY97.

Notes

1. The NLSY79 interviews in 1987 were conducted from March to October, with 72 percent conducted from April to June. The NLSY97 interviews in 2004–2005 were conducted from October 2004 to July 2005, with 76 percent conducted between November 2004 and January 2005. To obtain consistently measured education and employment outcomes, ideally sample members across these cohorts would be interviewed during the same time of year. The approximate five-month difference in age between the two cohorts implies that changes over time in educational attainment and employment outcomes will be biased downwards. But we control for sample member age as well as month of interview in all regressions, which should minimize any bias.
2. Since 5.3 percent unemployment was achieved in 1989–1990 without any appreciable growth of inflation, most would regard that as approximately the Non-Accelerating Inflation Rate of Unemployment (or NAIRU) for the 1980s. In the period 1999–2000, a rate of 4.0 percent unemployment was similarly achieved. But since some positive supply shocks were benefiting the economy and likely dampening inflation at that time (Blinder and Yellen 2001), a rate somewhat closer to 4.5 percent might be more appropriately considered the NAIRU for the post-2000 decade. This is just mildly below the monthly rates of unemployment through the early months of 2007.
3. Nine sample members ages 22–24 at the time of the interview in 1987 and nine at the time of the interview in 2004–2005 were enrolled in high school. It was not possible to determine the type of college (two- or four-year) for 39 sample members interviewed in 1987 and for four interviewed in 2004–2005. We drop these sample members because we control for educational enrollment and attainment in the regressions later in the chapter, distinguishing between two- and four-year colleges.
4. We identify such individuals using the type of residence variable in the 1986 or 1987 interviews of the NLSY79 and the type of dwelling variable in the Round 7 (2003–2004) or the Round 8 (2004–2005) interview of the NLSY97.
5. When observed wages were nonzero, but less than $2 or greater than $50, the value for this variable is set to "missing."
6. See Abraham (2003) for a discussion of these issues, and BLS (2008) for further information. The CPI-U-RS eliminates some, though not all, of the upward bias in the CPI. Over the relevant time period, it is comparable to the Gross Domestic Product (GDP) Deflator for Personal Consumption Expenditures, which has been used by others (for example, Katz and Autor 1999) in analyzing real wage trends.
7. Some values were imputed using information about enrollment status and education level at the time of the interview in rounds prior to and following these November dates.
8. Though there might be some value to the GED degree, we regard those with GEDs as being closer to high school dropouts than to graduates in their educational attainment (Cameron and Heckman 1993).

9. High school graduates who might have attended college briefly but who have not completed at least one year are coded as having no postsecondary educational attainment.

10. While GPAs are available for the NLSY79, we do not report them here because making comparisons across time may be problematic due to possible differences in grading (not necessarily performance) over time. Armed Forces Qualification Test (AFQT) scores (not adjusted by age) are available for the 1979 cohort, while ASVAB scores (adjusted by age) are available for the 1997 cohort. Because the AFQT and ASVAB are not directly comparable, we also do not examine changes over time for these tests.

11. Substance use and unmarried childbearing could be measured by a certain age (e.g., age 18) or up until the most recent survey date. We chose to present the substance use results before age 18, since early use of these substances likely conveys more information about risky behavior than does later use. In contrast, childbearing out of wedlock is likely to have consequences for both mothers and children even for those giving birth beyond the teen years, as the literature reviewed in the previous chapter indicates. But the racial differences and trends over time presented in this chapter are not sensitive to the age cutoffs used in either case.

12. We examine crime and incarceration for the 1997 cohort only, because the NLSY79 did not collect information about these activities during the high school years.

13. Classical measurement error in independent variables, which is uncorrelated with other observed characteristics, tends to generate downward biases (toward zero, in absolute value) in estimated coefficients. The errors in measurement of the relevant variables in these models, such as underreporting of criminal activity, might not have that characteristic, and thus might generate biases that are harder to ascertain. Classical measurement error in dependent variables creates imprecise estimates rather than bias; if the error is not classical, however, both problems might result.

14. For the findings in this section, sample weights are used in the summary statistics but not in the regression analyses.

15. Though we do not report standard errors in the summary tables for Chapter 2, any differences that we discuss in the text are at least marginally significant. We do not show results of significance tests in the table because of the large number of possible tests of interest.

16. These gaps may not persist, however, with appropriate controls such as work experience and childbearing. For example, using the NLSY79, Waldfogel (1998) notes that young women without children have achieved rough parity with young men in hourly wages, though gaps remain between men and women with children.

17. Among Hispanics in the NLSY79 and NLSY97, the percentage not born in the United States has not changed substantially (about 20 percent in each cohort). Whether immigrant children are underrepresented in the more recent cohort (because there are more immigrants in the population) is not clear.

18. Among young black men who are not incarcerated, hours and weeks worked for the latter cohort are 1,478 and 39.2, respectively.

19. Turner shows that the lengthening time to degree is much stronger among those

from lower-to-middle-income families, suggesting that rising college costs and family income constraints are more important determinants of this trend than simply a growing taste for lengthier college spells among the young.

20. See also Holzer, Offner, and Sorensen (2005), Raphael (2007), and Western (2006) for evidence on the relationship between incarceration and employment among young black men.

21. Each regression also includes indicators for month of interview to control for time of year effects and age differences across sample members at the time of interview.

22. The models in this table also control for age and month of interview.

23. The age range of youth considered by Johnson and Neal is 26–31, and the authors focus on labor market outcomes observed in the early 1990s.

24. This result is stronger for women than for men when the samples are split by gender.

25. All else being equal, black males and females who have been incarcerated but are no longer incarcerated at the time of the Round 8 interview worked 4.3 fewer weeks in the year preceding the Round 8 interview. Black males worked 4.0 fewer weeks (not statistically significant), while black females worked 7.6 fewer weeks.

26. Chow tests indicate that the results for all blacks are significantly different from those for whites and Hispanics, while the separate results for black males versus black females are not significantly different from each other at the 0.05 level.

3
Household Structure and
Young Adult Outcomes

Chapter 2 documented gaps in employment and educational outcomes between white and minority young adults that have persisted or grown over the past few decades, with outcomes for young black men worsening in relative (or even absolute) terms. One potential explanation for the persistence of these gaps is the increasing likelihood that minority children grow up in single-parent families. The disadvantages associated with doing so may offset any progress they otherwise would have experienced. Such an explanation would, of course, imply that some part of the relationship between household structure and outcomes is causal, not simply reflecting other unobserved disadvantages that are correlated with growing up with a single parent.

In this chapter we examine household structure and its statistical relationship with observed outcomes among youth. Using information from the NLSY97, we show the range of household structures youth lived in when they were 12 years old, and how these differ by race. We show how household structure is correlated with other important characteristics of families and households, such as family income and parental education. Next the chapter presents estimates of the statistical associations between household structure and the outcomes that were introduced in Chapter 2 in areas of employment, education, and risky behaviors. These are based on regression equations that control for many characteristics of the young people and their mothers, including some that have been unobserved in previous work.

We show the extent to which relationships between household structure and outcomes can be attributed to differences in family income, and the extent to which racial differences in outcomes can be attributed to household structure. Focusing on young blacks, we calculate the extent to which changing household structure over time may be related to observed changes in their employment, educational, and behavioral outcomes. Finally, we explore the extent to which our estimated relationships may be causal by estimating fixed-effects models (comparing siblings at the same age within a household, and comparing the same individual over time).

Overall, the findings in this chapter indicate that household structure is strongly related to a range of observed outcomes, particularly in the areas of education and risky behaviors. Differences in household structure can account for a significant part of the differences between young white and black men on some outcomes. Furthermore, our evidence suggests that household structure can account for part of the persistence or worsening of outcomes over time for young black men. The fixed-effects models, despite their inherent limitations, also suggest that at least some parts of the estimated effects of household structure are causal.

SAMPLE AND MEASURES

The analyses in this chapter incorporate respondents of all ages in the NLSY97, though we have restricted the sample to the largest racial and ethnic subgroups: white non-Hispanics, black non-Hispanics, and Hispanics. We examine seven outcome measures, introduced in Chapter 2 and described again below, measured in Round 8 (October 2004 to July 2005).

The two new measures introduced in this chapter are household structure and parental income. To measure household structure, we create a set of mutually exclusive indicators of whether the sample member at age 12 lived with

- both biological parents
- a mother who had never been married
- a mother who had been married but did not currently have a spouse in the household
- a mother and her spouse (not the sample member's father)
- a father (with or without a spouse who was not the sample member's mother)
- some other family arrangement (including foster or adoptive parents, or grandparents).

This measure is defined using information from created variables in the NLSY97 file, as well as from the parent respondent's marital history collected in the survey's first round.

We do not create a separate category for unmarried parents who cohabit, because these households constitute a relatively small fraction of each category except the last one.[1] In addition, the literature on cohabiters suggests that these unions are often unstable in the United States, and that outcomes for youth in these families do not differ dramatically from those for the children of other unmarried parents over time (Acs 2006; Wu and Wolfe 2001).

Our measure of household structure reflects not only point-in-time status when the sample member was 12 years old but also some history, as reflected in whether the mother has never married, or was previously married and has or has not remarried. Because the outcomes we investigate likely reflect parental supervision and involvement recently for adolescents and teens as well as the earlier cognitive and social development of children and youth over time, a household structure measure that takes both point-in-time and history into account is appropriate. Because it is not possible to construct a similar variable in the NLSY79 that accounts for this historical aspect of the parental relationship, a comparison over time of these categories is not possible.

We chose to measure household structure at age 12 because it could be measured relatively consistently for all sample members and because it reflected the youth's household at an early point in his or her teen years. Transition matrices of household structures from age 2 to age 12, and from age 12 to age 16 (Tables A.3 and A.4, found in Appendix A) show relative stability over these time spans for sample members who lived with both biological parents or with a never-married mother. Greater transitions occurred between the categories of 1) mothers who had been married but had no spouse in the household and 2) mothers who lived with their spouses. Thus, we have most confidence in our inferences of relationships to outcomes of household structures when we measure households with both biological parents and those with never-married mothers.

Of course, many alternative measures of household structure are of interest, including ones that reflect additional detail in the structure at a point in time (for example, specifying households that include grandparents or parents' cohabiters), household structure at other ages or multiple points in time, or instability in household structure experienced by a child or young adult (Aughinbaugh, Pierret, and Rothstein 2005; DeLeire and Kalil 2002; Kamp Dush and Dunifon 2007; Pierret 2001; Sandefur and Wells 1999). We acknowledge the utility of these alternative and additional measures and encourage their use in future research. Our focus in the current work, however, is less on exploring the many (and important) variants of household structure and more on documenting how a particular measure of structure is related to a broad range of young adult outcomes—most importantly, how these relationships differ by race and gender.

Another important measure introduced in this chapter is parental income. We construct this as a two-year average of income as measured when the youth was 14 and again at 15 years old (for sample members born in 1982–1984) or an average of income at 16 and 17 (for sample members born in 1980–1981).[2] This is a measure of parental income (not total household income), drawn from the parent interview in Round 1, as well as the income updates through the fifth round of the survey. A single measure that combines two-year averages at different ages is not ideal; however, we use this measure because measuring parental income and household structure at similar time points is desirable, and a two-year average is preferred over a one-year measure because it can smooth out transitional changes that might occur in any particular year. Balancing these criteria led us to use the measure of parental income just described.[3] Even with the two-year average, this measure may be subject to considerable measurement error because the income elements were gathered in only a few questions and were self-reported (making recall of specific values difficult).

Other measures used as controls in the regression equations are described in the next section.

ESTIMATED EQUATIONS

We estimate a series of reduced-form regression equations using Ordinary Least Squares (OLS) of the following form:

$$(3.1) \quad Y_i = f(HH_i, X_i, M_i) + \eta_i,$$

where Y refers to each of seven outcomes of interest for young adult i: two labor market outcomes (the "natural log of hourly wages" and "weeks worked" over the previous year), two for educational attainment ("high school dropout or GED" and "enrolled in a four-year college or earned a bachelor's degree"), one for scholastic achievement ("ASVAB test percentile score"), and two for risky or illegal behaviors ("having a child outside of marriage" and "ever being incarcerated"). Standard errors are adjusted to account for the clustering of youth within households. We chose this set of outcomes from the broader set in Chapter 2 to make the analysis more tractable, and to focus more particularly on the most reliable measures. Thus, we focus on ASVAB test scores rather than self-reported GPA, since the former is more objective and is measured more uniformly across respondents, and we also focus on incarceration rather than self-reported crime, since the former is at least partially measured objectively (when interviews are conducted in prison) and is much less subject to any self-report bias than the latter.

The independent variables of primary interest in these regressions are the HH variables, which refer to household structure at age 12 as defined above (living with both biological parents is the omitted category). X refers to control variables for sample member characteristics: age, race, gender, number of siblings in the household when the youth was 16 years old,[4] and the month of the Round 8 interview. Finally, M refers to control variables for characteristics of the sample member's mother: age at the birth of her first child, whether she was born in the United States; hours worked in 1996 (whether she worked less than 20 hours, 20 to 34 hours, or 35 or more hours a week); and educational attainment in terms of whether she was a dropout (or had a GED), had a high school diploma, associate's degree, or bachelor's degree or higher (obtained from the youth retrospectively in Rounds 6 to 8). This set of controls is quite extensive relative to those used in previous work, with measures like maternal employment that likely capture attitudes towards work and responsibility (among other factors).[5]

A second specification for each of the seven outcomes adds parental income to the variables included in the previous equation:

$$(3.2) \quad Y_i = f(HH_i, X_i, M_i, I_i) + \varepsilon_i,$$

where I refers to a set of parental income quintile dummies, which allow for nonlinearities in the effects of income.

In addition to the OLS regressions estimated in Equations 3.1 and 3.2, we also estimate two types of fixed-effects models in an attempt to estimate the causal effect of household structure on outcomes. The first type of fixed-effect model uses siblings to examine differences in household structure at age 12 across individuals and consequent differences between them in the outcomes we observe in early adulthood; the other uses the same individuals to examine changes in household structures and outcomes over time. For the sibling fixed-effects models, we include information for all siblings in each household, their family structure at age 12, and their outcomes in Round 8 (2004–2005). For these models, the effects of household structure are identified by changes in structure across siblings at age 12.[6] For the individual fixed-effects models, we measure outcomes at Round 4 (2000–2001, when sample members were roughly 16 to 20 years old) and at Round 8 (2004–2005, when sample members were roughly 20 to 24 years old).[7] We also measure household structure in one set of the individual fixed-effects models with a two-year lag and in another set with a three-year lag, because it is unlikely that changes in household structure over time for the same person will instantaneously translate into differences in the kinds of outcomes we consider.[8]

Both the sibling and individual fixed-effects models are meant to address the problem that omitted personal characteristics may be related both to household structure and to outcomes, thus biasing any household structure effects that are estimated by using ordinary least squares. The fixed-effects models attempt to address this concern by identifying the effect of household structure within families or individuals—either across siblings or over time for a particular sample member—thus removing any unobserved factors related to the family or individual that may bias OLS estimates.

The fixed-effects strategy is not a panacea, however, as some serious limitations arise for identifying effects of household structure with these data. First, changes across time in some categories can only happen in a single direction; for instance, it is possible only for an older sibling or for an individual at the first time point to have a "never married" mother. Second, the measures of household structure may not be sufficiently far apart to observe much variation for identifying the models. Siblings in this data set are, on average, only two years apart in age, and the individual fixed-effects model measures household income just four years apart. If household structure influences youth behaviors and outcomes through the longer term, then these short-term changes in household structure are insufficient for identifying their effect. Taken all together, these limitations suggest that the fixed-effect estimates will likely be biased toward zero.[9]

EMPIRICAL RESULTS

This section presents basic descriptive statistics on household structure, family income, and mother's educational attainment.[10] The next section presents results from regressions predicting the seven key outcomes, focusing on explanatory effects of household structure and race. Also presented here are results from the two sets of fixed-effects models.

Descriptive Statistics

Table 3.1 shows the distribution of household structures of youth at age 12 in the NLSY97, for the entire sample and separately by race. Only about half of all youth lived with both biological parents at age 12. Among the remainder of the sample, about two-thirds (or one-third of the overall sample) lived with a mother who was either currently married to someone other than the youth's father or who had been married in the past (but did not currently live with her spouse). Only about 6 percent of all youth lived at age 12 with a mother who had never been married, and just over 10 percent lived either with their fathers only or with other adults (including grandparents or foster parents).

Comparing across racial groups, Hispanic youth in the sample were in households broadly similar in structure to those of young whites, though with a somewhat higher percentage of never-married mothers (about 7 versus 2 percent, respectively). In contrast, young blacks are much more likely than young whites or Hispanics to live in households with never-married mothers: roughly one-fifth of all young blacks at age 12 lived with mothers who had never been married. Almost one-fourth of young blacks lived with mothers who were currently married to men other than the sample members' own fathers, and just under a

Table 3.1 Household Structure at Age 12, Total and by Race (%)

	All races	Whites	Blacks	Hispanics
At age 12, sample member lived with				
Both biological parents	50.93	57.32	20.21	52.02
Mother, never married	5.70	2.14	20.92	7.39
Mother, had been married, no spouse in household	14.74	13.82	18.47	15.46
Mother and her spouse	18.30	17.53	23.56	16.19
Father	4.81	4.91	4.69	4.33
Other	5.53	4.27	12.15	4.61
Sample size	7,323	3,910	1,908	1,505

NOTE: Sample includes all available NLSY97 respondents.
SOURCE: Authors' tabulations from NLSY97.

fifth (18 percent) lived with mothers who had been married but did not have a spouse in the household. Just over one-fifth of young blacks lived with both biological parents at age 12. Finally, about 5 percent of young blacks lived with their fathers only (a comparable percentage to those of young whites and Hispanics), while about 12 percent lived with other adults (a higher percentage than whites or Hispanics).

Though these are cross-sectional results, other sources (such as the census or the Current Population Survey) have documented growth over time in single parenthood (especially from the 1960s through the 1980s) among all racial groups, and especially among blacks. For instance, the 1960 decennial census indicated that only 2 percent of black children lived with a never-married parent, while 67 percent lived with a married couple, who in the vast majority of cases were their own biological parents (Ellwood and Crane 1990).[11]

The very high incidence of single parenthood in the black community and its rise over time suggest that at least part of the persistence of large gaps in educational and employment outcomes (as well as participation in risky behaviors) between young blacks and others might be attributable to these changes in family background. Effects of household structure are likely to reflect differences in household income, which (all else being equal) should be lower in single-parent than in two-parent families. It is also likely that differences in household income—and, more broadly, in youth outcomes and behaviors—are attributable to other characteristics of youth and their families that are correlated with household income but not necessarily caused by it.

In the next two tables we show summary statistics, conditional on household structure, for average family income (Table 3.2) and mother's educational attainment (Table 3.3). Table 3.2 shows that the average family incomes of youth are strongly correlated with their household structures. In particular, the average annual parental income of young people who live with both biological parents is highest, at almost $74,000 per year. In contrast, those living with divorced or remarried mothers, or with fathers or other adults, have family incomes that are 46 to 64 percent lower (i.e., approximately $34,000 to $47,000 per year). And those living with never married mothers have by far the lowest of all family incomes, averaging about $19,000 per year.

We find similar patterns within each racial group, but a few notable differences across the groups. Family income for young blacks and Hispanics is lower, on average, than for whites, regardless of household structure. For instance, blacks or Hispanics living with both biological parents have family incomes only 58 to 63 percent of family incomes for white youth. Within other categories of household structure, family income for blacks and Hispanics is lower than for white youth by

Table 3.2 Average Family Income for Various Household Structures, Total and by Race ($)

	All races	Whites	Blacks	Hispanics
At age 12, sample member lived with				
Both biological parents	73,785	79,785	50,005	46,222
Mother, never married	19,277	28,760	15,180	17,030
Mother, had been married, no spouse in household	34,340	40,119	22,078	22,127
Mother and her spouse	47,033	53,822	31,762	32,267
Father	45,372	48,661	33,732	39,391
Other	38,962	52,693	20,130	26,374
Sample size	6,675	3,393	1,818	1,464

NOTE: Family income is a two-year average of parental income when the youth turned 14 to 15 years old (for sample members born in 1982–1984) or 16 to 17 (for sample members born in 1980–1981). Created from parent interviews in Round 1 and income updates through Round 5.

SOURCE: Authors' tabulations from NLSY97.

comparable amounts. But young blacks growing up with never-married mothers have the lowest family incomes of any group, at roughly $15,000 per year, well under one-third of family income for black youth in households with both biological parents—the greatest relative gap among any two household categories within any racial group.

If anything, the association between household structure and family income may be understated here because of the differences in timing between the measurement of household structure and that of family income, and by reporting errors, as noted earlier. Nevertheless, these associations imply that household income is likely to be an important mechanism through which parental structure affects youth and young adult outcomes. Prior research has documented relationships between household income and a wide range of outcomes observed among children, youth, and adults; debates remain, however, over the extent to which these effects are driven by income itself or by other attributes of households that are correlated with income (Duncan 2005; Mayer 1997). Also open to question is the degree to which differences in household structure cause differences in family income, or whether differences in income are simply reflective of other personal characteristics that drive both structure and income.

The strong association between household structure and maternal educational attainment is shown in Table 3.3. Among youth living with never-married mothers, about one-third of their mothers are high school dropouts (or had a GED). In contrast, among sample members living with both biological parents, only one-tenth of their mothers are high school dropouts. Maternal education for other household structures falls somewhere in between. Similarly, among youth who live with both biological parents, more than 30 percent of their mothers have at least a bachelor's degree, while only 8 percent of mothers in the never-married category do. In results available from the authors, similar patterns can also be observed within each racial group, though the dropout rate for mothers of black youths living in never-married-mother households is somewhat lower than that of white or Hispanic youth.[12]

The strong association between household structures and maternal education implies that some of the observed relationships between those structures and other outcomes among youth might be spurious. The fact that we can measure maternal background and characteristics, and can control for these in regression analysis, means that these correla-

Table 3.3 Household Structure at Age 12, by Mother's Educational Attainment (%)

	Dropout/ GED	High school diploma	Associate's degree	Bachelor's degree or more	Total
At age 12, sample member lived with					
Both biological parents	11.04	46.54	11.76	30.66	100
Mother, never married	34.39	50.20	7.17	8.24	100
Mother, had been married, no spouse in household	19.01	47.73	12.69	20.57	100
Mother and her spouse	20.84	47.61	13.66	17.88	100
Father	17.71	50.29	11.87	20.14	100
Other	28.25	50.08	8.91	12.77	100
Sample size	1,289	2,951	662	1,236	6,138

SOURCE: Authors' tabulations from NLSY97.

tions will not bias our estimates of the relationships between household structure and youth outcomes. However, other correlates of household structure might not be so easily observable (within our data or other data) and could potentially bias these estimates to a greater extent.

Regression Estimates for Seven Key Outcomes

Table 3.4 presents coefficient estimates from regression models predicting the seven key outcomes. For each outcome, two specifications (Equations 3.1 and 3.2) are estimated for each of four groups: 1) the full sample of white, black, and Hispanic young adults; 2) black males and females; 3) black males only; and 4) black females only. Thus, for each outcome, Table 3.4 reports eight estimates for each household structure category.

Overall, the results show that household structure is strongly correlated with almost every outcome considered here, even after controlling for a range of individual and maternal characteristics as well as for family income. Furthermore, the estimated effects of household structure for blacks are generally similar (in absolute magnitude) to those of the full sample. But, for some key measures, we find estimated effects for young black men that are greater than those for young black women or other groups.

Table 3.4 Effects of Household Structure on Outcomes, without and with Controls for Parental Income

	Natural log of hourly wage							
	Full sample		Blacks		Black males		Black females	
	(1)	(2)	(1)	(2)	(1)	(2)	(1)	(2)
Person or persons with whom sample member lived at age 12[a]								
Mother, never married	−0.042*	−0.016	−0.046	−0.018	−0.089*	−0.064	−0.022	0.008
	(0.022)	(0.023)	(0.035)	(0.035)	(0.048)	(0.048)	(0.051)	(0.052)
Mother, had been married, no spouse in household	−0.043**	−0.015	−0.050	−0.018	−0.080	−0.050	−0.030	0.002
	(0.020)	(0.021)	(0.036)	(0.037)	(0.054)	(0.056)	(0.050)	(0.052)
Mother and her spouse	−0.010	0.005	−0.056	−0.039	−0.060	−0.043	−0.054	−0.036
	(0.018)	(0.018)	(0.035)	(0.034)	(0.047)	(0.046)	(0.050)	(0.049)
Father	−0.011	0.003	0.000	0.017	−0.057	−0.029	0.024	0.032
	(0.036)	(0.036)	(0.059)	(0.060)	(0.065)	(0.066)	(0.105)	(0.109)
Other	−0.042	−0.022	−0.016	0.014	−0.024	0.007	−0.001	0.025
	(0.028)	(0.028)	(0.046)	(0.046)	(0.060)	(0.060)	(0.067)	(0.067)
Average family income included	no	yes	no	yes	no	yes	no	yes
Observations	5,849	5,849	1,493	1,493	679	679	814	814
R-squared	0.088	0.093	0.099	0.108	0.085	0.096	0.130	0.138

Weeks worked

Person or persons with whom sample member lived at age 12[a]	Full sample		Blacks		Black males		Black females	
	(1)	(2)	(1)	(2)	(1)	(2)	(1)	(2)
Mother, never married	-2.621***	-1.573	-2.334	-1.768	-4.808**	-3.257	-0.038	-0.228
	(1.014)	(1.047)	(1.552)	(1.631)	(2.255)	(2.335)	(2.163)	(2.263)
Mother, had been married, no spouse in household	-2.669***	-1.999**	-4.332***	-3.794**	-7.310***	-5.735**	-1.556	-1.928
	(0.761)	(0.789)	(1.609)	(1.665)	(2.386)	(2.431)	(2.224)	(2.309)
Mother and her spouse	-0.649	-0.312	-2.176	-1.871	-3.863*	-2.846	-0.479	-0.813
	(0.673)	(0.679)	(1.560)	(1.575)	(2.272)	(2.255)	(2.120)	(2.145)
Father	-0.280	-0.266	1.382	1.677	2.862	4.109	-3.286	-3.666
	(1.335)	(1.330)	(3.138)	(3.157)	(3.848)	(3.852)	(4.960)	(5.087)
Other	-2.894**	-2.344**	-3.206	-2.678	-7.286**	-5.533*	0.479	0.155
	(1.169)	(1.179)	(2.066)	(2.112)	(3.089)	(3.190)	(2.616)	(2.667)
Average family income included	no	yes	no	yes	no	yes	no	yes
Observations	7,085	7,085	1,942	1,942	910	910	1,032	1,032
R-squared	0.059	0.065	0.048	0.050	0.062	0.070	0.059	0.062

(continued)

Table 3.4 (continued)

| | High school dropout/GED | | | | | | | |
| | Full sample | | Blacks | | Black males | | Black females | |
	(1)	(2)	(1)	(2)	(1)	(2)	(1)	(2)
Person or persons with whom sample member lived at age 12[a]								
Mother, never married	0.158***	0.108***	0.124***	0.088**	0.144***	0.095*	0.112***	0.084**
	(0.023)	(0.024)	(0.033)	(0.034)	(0.049)	(0.053)	(0.040)	(0.042)
Mother, had been married, no spouse in household	0.140***	0.099***	0.110***	0.078**	0.139***	0.100**	0.085**	0.056
	(0.016)	(0.016)	(0.030)	(0.032)	(0.047)	(0.049)	(0.037)	(0.040)
Mother and her spouse	0.094***	0.071***	0.039	0.021	0.011	-0.010	0.062*	0.047
	(0.014)	(0.014)	(0.029)	(0.029)	(0.044)	(0.044)	(0.034)	(0.035)
Father	0.098***	0.085***	0.039	0.026	0.133	0.120	-0.061	-0.079
	(0.029)	(0.029)	(0.053)	(0.052)	(0.081)	(0.079)	(0.060)	(0.061)
Other	0.106***	0.074***	0.090**	0.061	0.104*	0.058	0.093**	0.073
	(0.024)	(0.024)	(0.039)	(0.040)	(0.060)	(0.063)	(0.047)	(0.048)
Average family income included	no	yes	no	yes	no	yes	no	yes
Observations	7,115	7,115	1,964	1,964	923	923	1,041	1,041
R-squared	0.138	0.154	0.155	0.164	0.156	0.169	0.167	0.176

Enrolled in four-year college or not enrolled, bachelor's degree or more

Person or persons with whom sample member lived at age 12[a]	Full sample		Blacks		Black males		Black females	
	(1)	(2)	(1)	(2)	(1)	(2)	(1)	(2)
Mother, never married	-0.164***	-0.119***	-0.153***	-0.109***	-0.124***	-0.117***	-0.183***	-0.105**
	(0.018)	(0.018)	(0.030)	(0.032)	(0.039)	(0.040)	(0.046)	(0.049)
Mother, had been married, no spouse in household	-0.152***	-0.100***	-0.114***	-0.072**	-0.112**	-0.110**	-0.120**	-0.038
	(0.016)	(0.016)	(0.033)	(0.035)	(0.044)	(0.045)	(0.051)	(0.053)
Mother and her spouse	-0.147***	-0.116***	-0.099***	-0.077**	-0.040	-0.041	-0.151***	-0.109**
	(0.015)	(0.015)	(0.033)	(0.033)	(0.045)	(0.045)	(0.047)	(0.048)
Father	-0.174***	-0.146***	-0.071	-0.056	-0.071	-0.078	-0.103	-0.061
	(0.028)	(0.027)	(0.059)	(0.058)	(0.076)	(0.077)	(0.098)	(0.093)
Other	-0.146***	-0.108***	-0.122***	-0.086**	-0.105**	-0.102**	-0.143***	-0.086
	(0.022)	(0.022)	(0.036)	(0.037)	(0.046)	(0.046)	(0.055)	(0.056)
Average family income included	no	yes	no	yes	no	yes	no	yes
Observations	7,115	7,115	1,964	1,964	923	923	1,041	1,041
R-squared	0.199	0.219	0.139	0.152	0.119	0.121	0.168	0.203

(continued)

66

Table 3.4 (continued)

	ASVAB							
	Full sample		Blacks		Black males		Black females	
	(1)	(2)	(1)	(2)	(1)	(2)	(1)	(2)
Person or persons with whom sample member lived at age 12[a]								
Mother, never married	-9.838***	-5.874***	-8.217***	-4.258**	-8.833***	-5.035**	-7.631***	-3.014
	(1.229)	(1.238)	(1.821)	(1.816)	(2.561)	(2.506)	(2.477)	(2.510)
Mother, had been married, no spouse in household	-7.621***	-3.869***	-7.456***	-3.502*	-9.625***	-6.043**	-5.461**	-0.866
	(1.005)	(1.028)	(1.933)	(1.933)	(2.718)	(2.658)	(2.701)	(2.752)
Mother and her spouse	-5.594***	-3.486***	-3.461*	-1.379	-3.199	-0.885	-3.883	-1.734
	(0.975)	(0.966)	(1.858)	(1.789)	(2.661)	(2.565)	(2.414)	(2.353)
Father	-5.704***	-4.152*	-3.747	-1.479	-1.586	0.579	-8.735*	-5.494
	(1.853)	(1.815)	(3.323)	(3.056)	(4.460)	(4.224)	(4.857)	(4.561)
Other	-6.857***	-4.298***	-5.356**	-2.108	-6.552**	-2.913	-5.061*	-2.040
	(1.504)	(1.506)	(2.210)	(2.228)	(3.038)	(3.074)	(3.050)	(3.114)
Average family income included	no	yes	no	yes	no	yes	no	yes
Observations	6,780	6,780	1,793	1,793	869	869	924	924
R-squared	0.328	0.346	0.206	0.240	0.178	0.214	0.246	0.282

	Full sample		Blacks		Black males		Black females	
Unmarried with a child								
	(1)	(2)	(1)	(2)	(1)	(2)	(1)	(2)
Person or persons with whom sample member lived at age 12[a]								
Mother, never married	0.105***	0.079***	0.089**	0.055	0.086*	0.068	0.098*	0.048
	(0.023)	(0.023)	(0.036)	(0.037)	(0.050)	(0.053)	(0.053)	(0.054)
Mother, had been married, no spouse in household	0.080***	0.056***	0.144***	0.109***	0.167***	0.151***	0.122**	0.069
	(0.015)	(0.016)	(0.036)	(0.037)	(0.052)	(0.053)	(0.052)	(0.054)
Mother and her spouse	0.072***	0.059***	0.065*	0.045	0.058	0.048	0.077	0.047
	(0.015)	(0.015)	(0.034)	(0.035)	(0.046)	(0.048)	(0.051)	(0.051)
Father	0.066**	0.056*	0.084	0.062	0.100	0.088	0.100	0.066
	(0.029)	(0.029)	(0.066)	(0.066)	(0.092)	(0.092)	(0.099)	(0.096)
Other	0.085***	0.067***	0.107**	0.077*	0.147**	0.128*	0.079	0.042
	(0.025)	(0.025)	(0.044)	(0.044)	(0.066)	(0.068)	(0.058)	(0.059)
Average family income included	no	yes	no	yes	no	yes	no	yes
Observations	7,129	7,129	1,960	1,960	918	918	1,042	1,042
R-squared	0.134	0.138	0.110	0.117	0.070	0.075	0.119	0.132

Table 3.4 (continued)

	Ever incarcerated							
	Full sample		Blacks		Black males		Black females	
	(1)	(2)	(1)	(2)	(1)	(2)	(1)	(2)
Person or persons with whom sample member lived at age 12[a]								
Mother, never married	0.075***	0.067***	0.079***	0.073***	0.149***	0.134***	0.019	0.019
	(0.014)	(0.014)	(0.018)	(0.019)	(0.035)	(0.037)	(0.015)	(0.015)
Mother, had been married, no spouse in household	0.047***	0.039***	0.054***	0.049***	0.078**	0.065**	0.037**	0.039**
	(0.010)	(0.010)	(0.018)	(0.018)	(0.031)	(0.032)	(0.016)	(0.018)
Mother and her spouse	0.050***	0.046***	0.040**	0.037**	0.054*	0.048	0.021	0.022
	(0.009)	(0.009)	(0.016)	(0.016)	(0.030)	(0.030)	(0.015)	(0.014)
Father	0.027	0.023	0.047	0.045	0.077	0.072	0.033	0.036
	(0.017)	(0.017)	(0.037)	(0.038)	(0.060)	(0.060)	(0.038)	(0.037)
Other	0.071***	0.066***	0.073***	0.069***	0.164***	0.151***	−0.003	−0.001
	(0.016)	(0.016)	(0.024)	(0.025)	(0.047)	(0.048)	(0.017)	(0.018)
Average family income included	no	yes	no	yes	no	yes	no	yes
Observations	7,208	7,208	2,028	2,028	981	981	1,047	1,047
R-squared	0.286	0.287	0.367	0.368	0.383	0.385	0.150	0.154

NOTE: Robust standard errors clustered by family are shown in parentheses. Variables are measured in Round 8 of the NLSY97, from October 2004 to July 2005. Average family income is measured from ages 14 to 15 for the 1982–1984 birth cohorts and from 16 to 17 for the 1980–1981 birth cohorts. Control variables include respondent's age at Round 8 interview, mother's age when she had her first child, whether mother is an immigrant, number of siblings in the respondent's household at age 16, mother's educational attainment, mother's hours worked, and month of Round 8 interview. Missing data dummies were included for all explanatory variables except for race/gender. Statistical significance is denoted as follows: * p < 0.10; ** p < 0.05; *** p < 0.01.
[a] The household structure category of sample members living with two biological parents is the omitted category in the regressions.
SOURCE: Authors' tabulations from NLSY97.

Results for the first outcome shown—the natural log of hourly wages—are an exception to the more general conclusion just stated: in these models, contrary to our general results, the estimated relationships between household structure and hourly wages are seldom statistically significant. The coefficients are generally negative (as predicted) but statistically significant in only three cases (all of which become insignificant when controlling for family income). The first two cases involve, for the full sample, young adults who lived at age 12 with mothers who either had never married or did not live with their spouses. In either case, these young adults earn up to 4 percent less than those who grew up with both biological parents. The third case involves black male youth living with a never-married mother; these youth had wages that were 9 percent lower.

The relationships observed between household structure and weeks worked is somewhat stronger. For instance, youth who lived with never-married or previously married mothers (as well as those living with other adults) generally work two to three fewer weeks per year than those who lived with both biological parents, which represents a substantively significant decline in work effort (relative to the mean of 39 weeks worked reported in Chapter 2).

But compared to these relatively weak associations with labor market measures, the estimated relationships between household structure and educational outcomes of youth, as well as between household structure and the tendency of youth to be unmarried with a child or ever incarcerated, are considerably stronger. In almost all cases, those growing up with any household structure (and especially with never-married mothers) other than two biological parents present have worse outcomes on average than those who are in households with both biological parents. The estimated partial correlations (controlling for several important characteristics of mothers and youth) are relatively large in many cases.

For instance, the results for the full sample indicate that the likelihood of being a high school dropout is 11 to 16 percentage points higher for those who lived with never-married mothers, 10 to 14 points higher for those who lived with previously married mothers, and 7 to 11 points higher for those who lived in some other situation. Given that dropouts constitute about 15 percent of all youth in this sample, these are very large estimated relationships. The likelihood of being enrolled in or having completed at least a four-year college degree is 10 to 17 percentage points lower for those youth who did not live with both biological parents than for those who did, relative to a mean of just under 30 percent. ASVAB percentile scores are, on average, 5.9 to 9.8 points lower for youth in never-married-mother households, and 3.5 to 7.6 points lower for those in other categories compared with having both biological parents present; these too constitute relatively large effects.

Youth who lived with never-married mothers are 8 to 11 percentage points more likely to have children of their own outside of marriage, while those in other categories are 6 to 9 percentage points more likely to do so than those growing up with both biological parents (relative to a mean of 19 percent for the sample). And those living with never-married mothers are 7 to 8 percentage points more likely to have been incarcerated at some point (recall that the sample mean was actually 6 percent).

Comparing coefficients across specifications 1 and 2 in Table 3.4 for each outcome shows some variation in the extent to which household income accounts for the estimated statistical relationships between household structure and outcomes. Typically, those estimated relationships are reduced by 25 percent or more. In some cases, the estimated magnitudes of the coefficients on household structure are reduced more substantially; for instance, up to 40 percent of the negative effects on weeks worked or ASVAB associated with growing up with a never-married mother are accounted for by reduced family income. Yet for most of the outcomes shown in Table 3.4, the estimated relationships with household structures remain substantively and statistically significant, even after controlling for parental income.

Measured family income here thus accounts for a bit less of the estimated effects of household structure than it has in some other studies (e.g., McLanahan and Sandefur 1994). Perhaps this reflects the extensive set of controls for maternal characteristics (including hours worked) contained in both specifications. It is also possible that the differences in timing and measurement error reduced the observed effects of income on these outcomes, though it is unlikely that either of these effects would be very large.[13] Most likely, the negative observed relationships between household structure and outcomes work through another set of mediating factors, which may or may not be causal.

Table 3.4 also shows the estimated relationships of household structure and each outcome, separately for blacks, black males, and black females. These comparisons provide insight into whether estimated effects for blacks (for whom the concentration of youth in single-parent households is greater) are different from those of whites and Hispanics. Most noteworthy is the general similarity of estimates (in magnitude) for blacks in Table 3.4 to those for the full sample—a finding consistent with earlier evidence from Haurin (1992), McLanahan and Sandefur (1994), and others.[14]

This is the case even though families without both biological parents present reach much further into the distribution of black families than of white or Hispanic families. As noted above (endnote 12), maternal educational attainment of black youth in never-married-mother households is somewhat greater than for white or Hispanic youth, as more black women fall into that category. And yet it appears that the estimated consequences of such parenthood for black youth may be just as negative as for youth of other races. When combined with the much greater incidence of single parenthood in black families, these findings suggest important effects of household structure on outcomes for young blacks relative to other groups and over time, as we indicate below.

Furthermore, estimates of household structure on outcomes separately for black males and black females are generally similar to those of the full sample. Notable exceptions are observed in the relationships with weeks worked and with incarceration, in which the estimated effects for black men are much larger than those for black women or other groups. The results thus imply that the deteriorating employment rates and rising incarceration rates of young black men over time reflect, at least to some extent, their much greater tendencies to grow up with single parents.

To focus on some key results from Table 3.4, coefficient estimates are presented graphically for a subset of four outcomes. First, results from regressions predicting the outcome of high school dropout/GED are shown in Figure 3.1, Panel A. Specifically, the figure shows coefficient estimates (expressed in percentage points) for household structures of never-married mothers, and of mothers who had previously been married. Recall that the comparison group is the household structure of both biological parents. The estimates are shown for two specifi-

Figure 3.1 Effects of Household Structure on Outcomes, without and with Controls for Parental Income

Panel A: High school dropout/GED (percentage points)

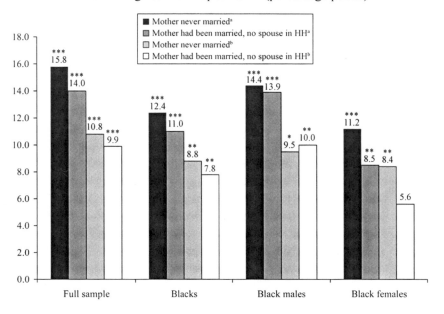

Panel B: Unmarried with a child (percentage points)

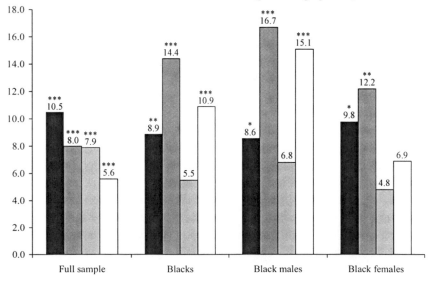

[a] Without controls for parental income.
[b] With controls for parental income.

Figure 3.1 (continued)

Panel C: Ever incarcerated (percentage points)

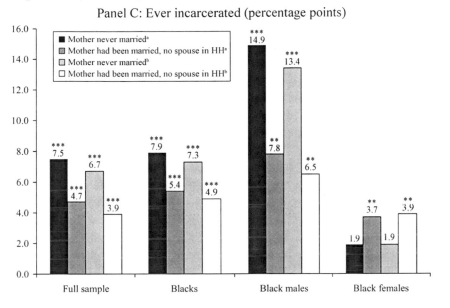

Panel D: Weeks worked (number of weeks)

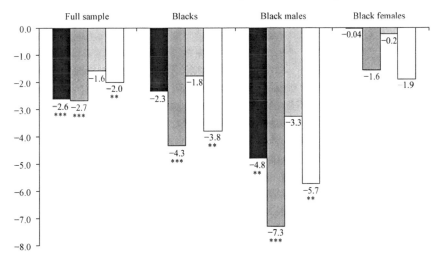

NOTE: Coefficients are from Table 3.4. Regression variables are measured in Round 8 of the NLSY97, from October 2004 to July 2005. Average family income is measured for ages 14 to 15 for the 1982–1984 birth cohorts and 16 to 17 for the 1980–1981 birth cohorts. Control variables include respondent's age at Round 8 interview, mother's age when she had her first child, whether mother is an immigrant, number of siblings in the respondent's household at age 16, mother's educational attainment, mother's hours worked, month of Round 8 interview, and respondent's household structure at age 12. Missing data dummies were included for all explanatory variables except for race/gender. Statistical significance is denoted as follows: * $p < 0.10$; ** $p < 0.05$; *** $p < 0.01$.

[a] Without controls for parental income.

[b] With controls for parental income.

cations (without and then with controls for parental income) separately for each of four samples (the full sample, blacks, black males, and black females). The same type of information is shown in the remaining panels of Figure 3.1, with Panel B showing estimates from regressions predicting whether the sample member was unmarried with a child, Panel C showing estimates from regressions predicting whether the sample member was ever incarcerated, and Panel D showing estimates from regressions predicting the number of weeks worked.

Observed differences in household structure, of course, may account for racial gaps in the employment, educational, and behavioral outcomes examined here. We address this issue in Table 3.5 for each of the seven outcomes. The first specification shows differences in outcomes by race and gender with no control for household structure but conditional on a number of sample member and maternal characteristics (listed in the table's endnote). Next, the second and third specifications show differences by race and gender, adding in household structure covariates (specification 2) and then adding controls for family income (specification 3). These latter two specifications correspond to those shown in Table 3.4 for the full sample.

Consistent with the findings in Chapter 2, Table 3.5 shows strong differences by race and gender in virtually every measured outcome, even when controlling for a number of individual and maternal characteristics in the first specification. Yet some outcome differences by race and gender can be largely accounted for by differences in household structure. For instance, differences in the likelihood of enrolling in and completing college between young white and black men largely disappear when we control for household structure.[15] Differences in dropping out of high school disappear once parental income is included as a control. Because the ability of household structure and income to account for racial differences in academic achievement (as measured by the ASVAB) appears more limited, their estimated effects on differences in educational attainment likely work through other mechanisms as well, such as youth attitudes or behaviors. The estimated effects of household structure on incarceration were large (Table 3.4), and they were consistent with the view that attitudinal and behavioral effects of single parenthood on youth are substantial; indeed, in Table 3.5 half or more of the racial differences among men are accounted for by including controls for household structure and parental income.

How much deterioration over time in employment, educational, and risky behavioral outcomes for blacks is predicted by the changes in family structure that have been observed since 1960—i.e., during the overall period in which family structure changed quite dramatically in the black community? We use estimates of these changes between 1960 and 1996, along with estimated coefficients from specification 1 for the black subsample in Table 3.4, to predict such changes.[16]

The results appear in Table 3.6. They suggest that the large changes over time in the structure of black households have only modestly affected labor market outcomes, reducing wages by about 2 percent and weeks worked by about one week. But the predicted changes in educational attainment and performance are larger. The calculations suggest that changes in household structure for blacks have added 4 percentage points to their high school dropout rates and reduced college attendance or completion by 5 percentage points, relative to means of 28 and 15 percent respectively for black males and 19 and 21 percent for black females, (Table 2.2).[17] The changes' effect on ASVAB percentile scores (2.7 points) is relatively modest in comparison to means among young blacks at roughly the thirtieth percentile (Table 2.3). They raise unmarried childbearing by about 4 percentage points (a somewhat modest increase in comparison to the black female mean of 48 percent or the black male mean of 31 percent shown in Table 2.4), but by adding over 2 percentage points to the incarceration rate of black men (at 15 percent in Table 2.5), they contribute a nontrivial amount to a costly phenomenon in the black community and in society.

Of course, there have been other, more positive developments in the family backgrounds of blacks in this time period (such as rising parental education and incomes) that have offset these predicted declines. But the results of Table 3.6 suggest that, absent the changes that occurred in black family structure between 1960 and 1996, the educational progress of the black community would have been significantly greater than it has been, while the rise in incarceration and participation in other risky behaviors among young blacks over time would not have been so great.

Table 3.5 Effects of Race on Outcomes, without and with Controls for Household Structure and Parental Income

	Natural log of hourly wage			Weeks worked			High school dropout/GED		
	(1)	(2)	(3)	(1)	(2)	(3)	(1)	(2)	(3)
Race/gender									
Black male	-0.105***	-0.093***	-0.075***	-7.538***	-6.886***	-6.207***	0.074***	0.035**	0.002
	(0.019)	(0.020)	(0.020)	(0.820)	(0.839)	(0.854)	(0.017)	(0.018)	(0.018)
Hispanic male	0.003	0.007	0.018	0.979	1.105	1.506*	0.022	0.014	-0.007
	(0.022)	(0.022)	(0.022)	(0.879)	(0.879)	(0.884)	(0.019)	(0.019)	(0.019)
White female	-0.162***	-0.161***	-0.162***	-1.975***	-1.936***	-1.928***	-0.024**	-0.028***	-0.029***
	(0.017)	(0.017)	(0.017)	(0.585)	(0.584)	(0.581)	(0.011)	(0.011)	(0.011)
Black female	-0.188***	-0.175***	-0.157***	-7.184***	-6.494***	-5.773***	-0.011	-0.052***	-0.086***
	(0.019)	(0.020)	(0.020)	(0.774)	(0.803)	(0.817)	(0.015)	(0.016)	(0.016)
Hispanic female	-0.140***	-0.135***	-0.121***	-4.525***	-4.267***	-3.807***	-0.040**	-0.053***	-0.077***
	(0.022)	(0.022)	(0.022)	(0.897)	(0.900)	(0.908)	(0.019)	(0.019)	(0.019)
Household structure included	no	yes	yes	no	yes	yes	no	yes	yes
Average family income included	no	no	yes	no	no	yes	no	no	yes
Observations	5,849	5,849	5,849	7,085	7,085	7,085	7,115	7,115	7,115
R-squared	0.087	0.088	0.093	0.056	0.059	0.065	0.119	0.138	0.154

	Enrolled in four-year college or not enrolled, bachelor's degree or more			ASVAB			Unmarried with a child		
	(1)	(2)	(3)	(1)	(2)	(3)	(1)	(2)	(3)
Race/gender									
Black male	-0.062***	-0.017	0.015	-22.709***	-20.309***	-17.751***	0.143***	0.116***	0.099***
	(0.016)	(0.016)	(0.017)	(1.053)	(1.086)	(1.081)	(0.017)	(0.017)	(0.017)
Hispanic male	-0.066***	-0.057***	-0.035*	-12.632***	-12.031***	-10.164***	0.053***	0.046***	0.035**
	(0.018)	(0.018)	(0.018)	(1.307)	(1.302)	(1.275)	(0.017)	(0.017)	(0.017)
White female	0.078***	0.083***	0.084***	2.047**	2.249***	2.229***	0.076***	0.073***	0.073***
	(0.015)	(0.014)	(0.014)	(0.835)	(0.829)	(0.822)	(0.011)	(0.011)	(0.011)
Black female	0.005	0.052***	0.083***	-8.601***	-16.092***	-13.539***	0.303***	0.274***	0.256***
	(0.017)	(0.017)	(0.017)	(1.045)	(1.081)	(1.076)	(0.017)	(0.017)	(0.018)
Hispanic female	-0.023	-0.011	0.015	-11.760***	-10.934***	-8.911***	0.162***	0.153***	0.140***
	(0.019)	(0.019)	(0.019)	(1.321)	(1.310)	(1.296)	(0.020)	(0.020)	(0.020)
Household structure included	no	yes	yes	no	yes	yes	no	yes	yes
Average family income included	no	no	yes	no	no	yes	no	no	yes
Observations	7,115	7,115	7,115	6,780	6,780	6,780	7,129	7,129	7,129
R-squared	0.177	0.199	0.219	0.316	0.328	0.346	0.126	0.134	0.138

(continued)

Table 3.5 (continued)

	Ever incarcerated		
	(1)	(2)	(3)
Race/gender			
Black male	0.045***	0.028**	0.023*
	(0.013)	(0.013)	(0.013)
Hispanic male	0.015	0.013	0.009
	(0.013)	(0.013)	(0.013)
White female	−0.049***	−0.050***	−0.050***
	(0.007)	(0.007)	(0.007)
Black female	−0.058***	−0.077***	−0.083***
	(0.009)	(0.009)	(0.010)
Hispanic female	−0.067***	−0.072***	−0.076***
	(0.010)	(0.010)	(0.011)
Household structure included	no	yes	yes
Average family income included	no	no	yes
Observations	7,208	7,208	7,208
R-squared	0.277	0.286	0.287

NOTE: Robust standard errors clustered by family are shown in parentheses. Variables are measured in Round 8 of the NLSY97, from October 2004 to July 2005. Average family income is measured from ages 14 to 15 for the 1982–1984 birth cohorts and from 16 to 17 for the 1980–1981 birth cohorts. Control variables include respondent's age at Round 8 interview, mother's age when she had her first child, whether mother is an immigrant, number of siblings in the respondent's household at age 16, mother's educational attainment, mother's hours worked, and month of Round 8 interview. Missing data dummies were included for all explanatory variables except for race/gender. "White male" is the omitted race/gender category in the regressions. For a description of specifications (1), (2), and (3), see bottom of p. 67/top of p. 68. Statistical significance is denoted as follows: * $p < 0.10$; ** $p < 0.05$; *** $p < 0.01$.
SOURCE: Authors' tabulations from NLSY97.

Table 3.6 Predicted Changes in Outcomes for Blacks over Time (1960–1996) Due to Changes in Family Structure

Person or persons with whom sample member lived at age 12	Natural log of hourly wage	Weeks worked	High school dropout/ GED	Enrolled in 4-year college or not enrolled, bachelor's degree or more	ASVAB	Unmarried with a child	Ever incarcerated
Mother, never married	−0.009	−0.452	0.024	−0.030	−1.592	0.017	0.015
Mother, had been married, no spouse in household	−0.005	−0.437	0.011	−0.012	−0.752	0.015	0.005
Mother and her spouse	−0.006	−0.232	0.004	−0.011	−0.369	0.007	0.004
Total	−0.020	−1.121	0.039	−0.053	−2.713	0.039	0.024

NOTE: Cell entries are equal to the product of the approximate percentage-point change over time in each household structure category (see endnote in the text) multiplied by the coefficient on household structure from column (1) for the category "Blacks" in Table 3.4.
SOURCE: Authors' tabulations from NLSY97.

Are the Estimated Effects of Household Structure Causal?

The estimated coefficients of Tables 3.4 and 3.5, and the predicted outcomes for blacks over time that appear in Table 3.6, imply substantial effects of household structure on a range of young adult outcomes. But the possibility remains that instead of being causal, these effects actually represent other unobserved characteristics of youth, their parents, and their households that are correlated with both household structure and the outcomes. While we use a more extensive set of control variables for other parental characteristics (including maternal weeks worked) than other studies, the likelihood remains that some important characteristics of parents or their children that are correlated with household structure are still unobserved.

Our preferred method of dealing with this possible problem is to estimate a series of fixed-effects models, based either on comparisons between siblings or on comparisons over time for the same individual (where multiple outcomes could be observed over time). The results of all these tests appear in Table 3.7. Instead of showing each estimated coefficient separately (the coefficients are mostly not statistically significant in these models anyway), we present the p-values for F tests on joint significance of the household structure variables. We also present two versions of the individual fixed-effects model, using either a two-year or a three-year lag between the points in time at which household structure and outcomes are measured for any individual. We do not control for household income in these equations.

The results for the sibling fixed-effects models show only two outcome equations in which the household structure variables remain jointly significant: those for being enrolled in or having completed a four-year college degree and those for ASVAB test score percentiles. These findings are consistent with the findings of Sandefur and Wells (1999), who found family structure effects on years of schooling using sibling fixed-effects models with data from the NLSY79.

Our fixed-effect results are somewhat stronger for the individual fixed effects: significant results (at least at the 0.10 level) appear for five out of six outcomes that could be measured over time using a two-year lag between observations of household structure and outcomes, and for three out of six using a three-year lag. Using either lag, we find significant effects of household structure on weeks worked and both

Table 3.7 Fixed-Effect Regressions with Controls for Mother's Background and Household Structure at Age 12

	Sibling regressions		Individual regressions			
	P-value for F-test of whether age 12 household structure dummies equal zero	Sample size	P-value for F-test of whether household structure at interview dummies (2-round lag) equal zero	Sample size	P-value for F-test of whether household structure at interview dummies (3-round lag) equal zero	Sample size
Natural log of hourly wage	0.150	1,998	0.502	4,397	0.773	4,397
Weeks worked	0.312	2,862	0.000***	6,658	0.000***	6,658
High school dropout/GED	0.559	2,880	0.051*	6,749	0.000***	6,749
Enrolled in four-year college or not enrolled, bachelor's degree or more	0.021**	2,880	0.000***	6,749	0.000***	6,749
ASVAB	0.000***	3,010				
Unmarried with a child	0.821	2,894	0.012**	5,380	0.424	5,380
Ever incarcerated	0.836	2,960	0.018**	6,627	0.217	6,627

NOTE: Robust standard errors are shown in parentheses. Variables are measured in Round 8 of the NLSY97, from October 2004 to July 2005. Control variables such as respondent's race/gender, respondent's age at Round 8 interview, mother's age when she had her first child, whether mother is an immigrant, number of siblings in the respondent's household at age 16, mother's educational attainment, mother's hours worked, and month of Round 8 interview were included but not reported in this table. Missing data dummies were included for all explanatory variables except for race/gender. Statistical significance is denoted as follows: * $p < 0.10$; ** $p < 0.05$; *** $p < 0.01$.
SOURCE: Authors' tabulations from NLSY97.

of our measures of educational attainment (i.e., dropping out of high school and attending or completing a degree at a four-year college). The shorter lag also generates significant effects of household structure on being unmarried with a child or being incarcerated.

In our view, the limitations of fixed-effects models for estimating these results likely lead to estimates that are biased toward a finding of no significant effect at all. In particular, the limitations are that a relatively small number of individuals or sibling pairs actually experience changes in household structure in the relevant time period (especially for the never-married mothers), and the time period during which any such changes can generate observable changes in behavior or outcomes is limited. Given that only two years in age separate the average pair of siblings in our data, it is perhaps not surprising that few significant results were observed for them; in contrast, the time periods over which differences are observed in the individual models are longer, at four years. But the fact that most of the individual fixed-effects in the two-year lag (and some in the other models) are significant suggests that at least some part of the estimated effects of household structure on youth outcomes is causal. Based on these estimates, however, it is very difficult to say exactly how much.

Our inability to pin down causal magnitudes more precisely here is a limitation of this work. Perhaps other estimation strategies, such as instrumental variables, might be more successful (though we note our own reservations about the use of these strategies to date in Chapter 1). Nevertheless, showing that at least some parts of our estimated effects are causal implies that the issue of household structure is a serious one, and thus it is important to understand more about exactly what are the mediating variables and mechanisms through which it works, as well as its potentially offsetting effects.

CONCLUSION

In this chapter, we present data on differences in household structure at age 12 for white, black, and Hispanic youth in the NLSY97. We also estimate the effects of household structure on a set of seven employment, educational, and behavioral outcomes and show differences by race. Finally, we estimate sibling and individual fixed-effects models to explore the extent to which the estimated effects are causal.

Our results suggest the following:

- Roughly one-half of all youth, and about four-fifths of black youth, do not live with both of their biological parents at age 12.

- Youth living without both biological parents, and especially with never-married mothers, are in households with substantially lower incomes when growing up, though this at least partly reflects other differences in parental characteristics (such as lower maternal education).

- Growing up without both biological parents is associated with modest reductions in wages and weeks worked for young adults, and more substantial reductions in educational attainment or achievement for them, as well as greater participation in risky or illegal behaviors.

- Lower family income accounts for less than half of these estimated effects in most cases.

- The greater tendency of young blacks to grow up in families without both biological parents, and especially with never-married mothers, accounts for fairly large parts of the racial differences in educational attainment and some risky behaviors among young men, and also for some of the limited progress (or actual deterioration) over time for blacks in these outcomes.

- Fixed-effects regression models for these outcomes—either across sibling pairs or over time for individuals—suggest that at least some part of the estimated relationships between household structure and these outcomes is causal, though we cannot infer the exact magnitudes.

Overall, the fact that large fractions of youth—especially black youth—grow up without both biological parents has negative implications for a range of outcomes during their teen and young adult years, especially those involving education and risky behaviors. Recent trends in household structure would appear to be at least partly responsible for the persisting black-white gaps in educational attainment and achievement, as well as the cycle of unmarried childbearing and dramatic increases in crime and incarceration that have affected black youth in general and young black men in particular. These findings are consistent with those of Sara McLanahan, Gary Sandefur, Daniel Lichter, Frank Furstenberg, and others noted in Chapter 1.

Some words of caution, however, are in order. For one, our analysis in this chapter does not explore the *causes* of household structure and its trends among blacks and other racial groups. A large literature does this elsewhere (see Chapter 1) and suggests that the causes of these trends lie partly in labor market changes (such as declining wages of less-educated men and rising relative wages of women) as well as in other demographic and attitudinal changes. Drawing firm conclusions about the possibly negative effects of these trends without understanding their causes might lead one to prematurely advocate for certain changes in behavior or policy that might not address the true causes.

Furthermore, it is likely—at least from the correlations we observe between household structure and maternal education—that some parts of the simple statistical relationships observed between household structures and outcomes are not causal. While we can easily control for maternal educational differences across individuals in our regression equations, we likely cannot observe or control for all of the relevant differences between youth or their parents that might affect these outcomes (such as the poorer families in which many single mothers themselves grew up). And while the various fixed-effects models we estimate seem to offer our best chance to account for these kinds of differences within these data, their limitations have also been clearly noted above.

It is also important to note that, despite the important effects of household structure on outcomes that we estimate, large racial gaps in most of these outcomes remain even after controlling for racial differences in household structure. This is particularly true for the large racial gaps in employment outcomes between young white and black men, but is also true for various gaps in educational achievement, unmarried parenthood, and incarceration. To note those parts of the gaps in outcomes for which we can account without acknowledging the parts for which we cannot account would be misleading.

Having stated these caveats, the task remains of gaining a better understanding of the mechanisms through which single parenthood negatively affects outcomes for youth and young adults, especially among blacks. If the disadvantages associated with growing up in single-parent families mostly do not stem from their lower incomes, as our findings seem to show, what other factors are at play? To what extent do these disadvantages grow out of parental attitudes and behaviors that might themselves be at least partial products of single parenthood? Are the true negative effects reinforced by other disadvantages—disadvantages associated with characteristics unique to the families or parents themselves or to the neighborhoods in which they live? At the same time, can these negative effects be offset by other choices and activities of parents, as Furstenberg et al. (1999) imply?

We turn to these questions in the next chapter.

Notes

1. For example, using additional information from the household rosters, we estimate that cohabiters make up just one-half of 1 percent of biological parent households and 5 percent of unmarried mother households (a combined category of never-married and previously married).
2. When only one year of income information was available, information from that year was used instead of setting the variable to missing.
3. We examined the correlations of single-year, two-year-average, and three-year-average income across different ages for available subsamples of youth. Single-year correlations ranged from 0.6 to 0.7, with higher correlations in concurrent years, as expected. Also as expected, correlations between two-year averages were higher (0.7 to 0.9), and correlations among three-year averages were highest (0.8 to 0.9).
4. Ideally, we would measure number of siblings in the sample member's household at the same time that household structure is measured (i.e., at age 12) or as close as possible to that age. Because of the age ranges of the youth initially surveyed, the age closest to age 12 at which we can measure number of siblings (including step and adoptive siblings) in the household, using the household rosters, is age 16.
5. The year 1996 corresponds to the time when sample members turned 12 to 16 years old. Whether maternal employment should be controlled for in all of these equations is debatable, if this measure is itself heavily affected by single-parent status. Our estimated outcome equations that do not include this control variable are qualitatively similar, but they do show somewhat greater effects of household income on the estimated household structure effects. These estimates are available from the authors upon request.
6. We also ran the models using household structure at age 6, but the results were not sensitive to this difference in timing.
7. Because it does not change over time, the outcome ASVAB is not estimated using individual fixed effects.
8. Our reduced-form OLS equations did not specify a particular time period during which household structure at age 12 should affect education, employment, and

behavioral outcomes among youth and young adults. But with individual fixed-effects models, these timing choices must be made more explicitly, because the exact timing of changes in household structure will now drive the changes in outcomes we seek to measure.

9. Of course, if the families that change household structure are not random, it is at least possible for the bias to go in the opposite direction.

10. Sample weights are used in the summary statistics, but not in the regression analyses.

11. Data from the NLSY79 and NLSY97 capture changes in household structure that occurred only during the 1980s and early 1990s. Additional tabulations show that the percentage of young blacks aged 14 to 18 at the time of the first survey round (1979 and 1997, respectively) who did not live with both biological parents rose from 59 percent to 73 percent between the two cohorts.

12. Among youth living with never-married mothers, 28.8 percent of black youth have mothers who were high school dropouts, compared with 38.5 percent of white youth and 46.1 percent of Hispanic youth.

13. The estimated influence of parental income was somewhat sensitive to the specific time period used. Part of the difficulty is that a consistent two-year (or greater) average family income cannot be calculated for all sample members across comparable years. Another part of the difficulty has to do with measurement error in the variable. Of all the parental income measures we examined for the full sample, the one we use in the estimated models has the greatest impact on reducing the effects of household structure.

14. In a few cases, the estimated effects for blacks are larger; these include the effects of having a never-married or a divorced-but-not-remarried mother on wages, and the effects of having a mother previously married but without a spouse on weeks worked and on the probability of having a child outside of marriage. In a variety of other cases, the estimated differences are a bit larger for the sample that includes whites and Hispanics. Most of these differences in estimated effects are only marginally significant at best, even though the Chow tests indicate statistically significant differences between equations estimated overall for blacks versus nonblacks.

15. Differences in educational attainment between white and black females can be inferred from comparisons between their coefficients (each measured relative to white males) and how the differences change across specifications. The racial difference in dropout behavior among young women is smaller than among young men, without and with the household controls, though the differences in college attendance or completion between young white and young black women are also narrowed significantly by these controls.

16. Our data on black family structure in 1960 are from Ellwood and Crane (1990). The family structure categories they use for describing the living arrangements of black children are "married couple," "divorced, separated, or widowed parent," "never-married parent," and "not with a parent." Comparing their numbers for 1960 (in Table 1) with ours for 1996 (Table 3.1, above), and making some assumptions about the gender distribution of their single-parent categories, we infer

that the fraction of black children living with both biological parents declined by roughly 40 percentage points (from about 0.60 to 0.20) and rose in the "never married," "divorced," and "remarried" mother categories by about 0.18, 0.10, and 0.12, respectively. The results in Table 3.7 are not very sensitive to small changes in the distribution of the 40-percentage-point decline.

17. The means for the latter category were obtained by summing the portions in the Table 2.2 categories for "not enrolled, bachelor's degree" and "enrolled, four-year college."

4

Other Correlates of Household Structure and Their Effects on Outcomes

The previous chapter showed strong statistical relationships between household structure and a range of employment, educational, and behavioral outcomes of young adults—both for the full sample and for the subgroup of blacks. While family income accounted for a considerable portion (up to 40 percent) of the effects of household structure on outcomes, significant portions remained, both statistically and substantively. Results from fixed-effects models suggested some causal role for household structure on outcomes, as well.

But how and why do household structures affect these outcomes? What are the mechanisms that account for the weaker performance of youth who have lived in single-parent households? Are these mechanisms themselves causal, and do they reflect causal effects of household structure? Or are they just spuriously related to household structure and to the outcomes themselves?

In this chapter, we further explore three types of household characteristics that are likely to be correlated both with household structure and with the employment, educational, and behavioral outcomes we examine. They are measures of 1) human capital enrichment, 2) parenting and home environment, and 3) neighborhood characteristics.

Using information from a subset of the NLSY97, we first show how measures in each of the three categories are associated with household structure. Next, we present regression models similar to those shown in Chapter 3, but now with these three types of household characteristics having been added. We show how the estimated effects of household structure differ once these characteristics are included in the models. We also show the joint influence of each of these three categories of variables on the outcomes.

The evidence presented in this chapter indicates that the three sets of household characteristics we examine do account for some of the statistical associations between household structure and outcomes. Furthermore, these characteristics themselves are associated statistically, and in some cases substantively, with the outcomes we examine. Thus, they help us better understand why the household structures in which young people grow up might affect their later outcomes in life, and they suggest how these effects might be addressed through policy interventions.

SAMPLE AND MEASURES

The analysis in this chapter uses a subsample of NLSY97 respondents born from 1982 to 1984, who were mostly ages 20 to 22 at the time of the Round 8 interview in 2004–2005. This sample restriction is necessary because some of the additional measures we analyze were collected (by survey design) only for these younger members of the cohort.

The NLSY97 collects a rich set of information about sample members' home and neighborhood environments and relationships with parents and peers.[1] We select a relatively small subset of 11 of these variables for further investigation in this chapter. These reflect the three overarching constructs of 1) human capital enrichment, 2) parenting and home environment, and 3) neighborhood characteristics.

We examine the extent to which the 11 variables reduce the estimated associations between household structure and the various outcomes, as well as the extent to which they themselves provide explanatory power for these outcomes.

There are good theoretical reasons for believing that these three sets of factors at least partly account for the observed effects of household structure on youth outcomes, as we note below. But, within each construct, we also had to choose from among a wide variety of variables in the NLSY that were conceptually similar and often fairly highly correlated with one another. As described further below, we selected 11 variables in all that had face validity for representing each construct, were not too strongly correlated with each other, and were related to the outcomes we examined (individually and as a group).

Our intent was not, as has been successfully done elsewhere (Child Trends 1999), to develop or use a composite index for different constructs, but instead to select a few representative measures in each area that would be reasonable and readily interpretable. We acknowledge the limitations of some of these measures and encourage future research that would refine the measures and further investigate their relationships with household structure and the range of outcomes presented here. Our work should thus be viewed as exploratory, rather than definitive, in some ways.

Why should these three sets of measures be related both to household structure and to youth outcomes? Regarding human capital, it appears that access to enriching and material resources early in life may promote positive youth development and directly or indirectly influence outcomes in early adulthood (e.g., Beltran, Das, and Fairlie 2006). To reflect such human capital enrichment, we use three self-reported measures (variables 1 through 3) from the 1997 Round 1 of the NLSY97 (when respondents were generally 12 to 14 years old):

1) whether there was usually a computer in the home in the previous month,

2) whether there was a dictionary in the home in the previous month, and

3) whether the youth spent any time taking extra classes or lessons.[2]

Regarding parenting and the home environment, the literature points to the importance of parents' support of, connection to, and regulation of their children (Barber and Olsen 1997; Dornbusch et al. 1987; Eccles et al. 1997; Slicker 1998; Steinberg et al. 1992; Tepper 2001). Regulation includes monitoring or setting limits, as well as offering or imposing structure through activities such as enrolling the children in extracurricular classes or doing things together as a family. Furthermore, the physical home environment—specifically, the orderliness of the home—is related to educational and labor market outcomes, suggesting that parents can influence noncognitive factors as well (Dunifon, Duncan, and Brooks-Gunn 2001). With variables 4 though 9, we examine six measures of parenting and home environment, all self-reported by the youth in Round 1 except where noted below. We measure:

4) how supportive the youth perceived his or her mother or mother figure to be (originally measured on a three-point scale, which we standardized to have a mean of zero and variance of one so that a one-unit increase in the variable corresponds with a one-standard-deviation increase);

5) whether the youth perceived his or her mother to be strict (compared to being permissive);

6) how much the youth thought his or her mother knew about whom the youth was with when the youth was not at home (measured on a five-point Likert scale, which we standardized to have a mean of 0 and a variance of 1);

7) how well-kept the interior of the youth's home was (as assessed by the interviewer on a three-point Likert scale, which we standardized to have a mean of 0 and variance of 1);

8) the number of days in a typical week that housework got done when it was supposed to; and

9) the number of days during a typical week that the family ate dinner together (a measure of structure).[3]

Finally, the quality of the physical and social neighborhood in which children and youth grow up may also affect their development and their future opportunities (Sampson, Raudenbush, and Earls 1997; Wilson 1987). With variables 10 and 11, we examine two measures of neighborhood quality from Round 1 of the NLSY:[4]

10) the number of days a week that gunshots are *not* usually heard (self-reported by the sample member);[5] and

11) a measure of how well kept buildings were in the neighborhood where the youth lived (a subjective rating on a three-point Likert scale by the interviewer, standardized to have a mean of 0 and variance of 1).

For each of these three overarching constructs, there is reason to believe that these measures will be correlated with household structure as well as youth outcomes. For instance, single parents who themselves are less educated and have weaker cognitive achievement might expose their children to less human capital enrichment; their lower incomes and other social ties might cause them to live in poorer neighborhoods;

and they might be less able to supervise their children and maintain orderly households, given the pressures of work and the instability of their lives. Clearly, some of these correlations with household structure might be spurious (especially those relating to human capital enrichment), some might reflect the lower incomes of these households (like enrichment and neighborhood quality), and others might be truly causal (especially those reflecting parenting and the home environment). With these expectations, we turn to the estimation and empirical results.

ESTIMATED EQUATIONS

Following McLanahan and Sandefur (1994), Furstenberg et al. (1999), and others, we build on the model specifications of Chapter 3 to now add the human capital, parenting and home environment, and neighborhood variables just described:

$$(4.1) \quad Y_i = f(HH_i, X_i, M_i, I_i, W_i) + \varepsilon_i,$$

where Y, HH, X, M, and I are all defined as they were in Chapter 3. W represents the set of household characteristics related to human capital enrichment, parenting and home environment, and neighborhood characteristics. We control for family income and other characteristics in Equation (4.1). Even so, the observed relationships between household structure and these household characteristics may be spurious.

We acknowledge, of course, that the estimated effects of these three sets of additional explanatory variables—like those of household structure—are not necessarily causal. Instead, we aim to produce a set of conditional estimates of household structure and household characteristics, related to a range of young adult outcomes. These estimates illustrate the potential mediating effects of these characteristics, and they also provide a sense of any remaining effects of household structure on these outcomes. But in the next section we also consider some reasons why these estimated effects might in part reflect causal relationships.

EMPIRICAL RESULTS

This section first presents descriptive statistics on the 11 household characteristics just described, separately by household structure for the full sample as well as for the subgroup of black sample members. Next, results from regression analyses that include these measures are presented.[6]

Descriptive Statistics

Sample means for each of the 11 variables are shown in Table 4.1, separately by household structure, both for the full sample and for the black subgroup.[7]

Each of the measures of human capital enrichment, parenting, and neighborhood characteristics shows clear associations with household structure. For example, over 70 percent of all youth with both biological parents present report having a computer in the home, while only about 21 percent of youth in households with never-married mothers do so. Forty-two to 57 percent of youth living in other types of households generally report the presence of computers. Similar patterns are observed for other enrichment measures, though with somewhat less variation across the household categories. For instance, over 90 percent of youth in each household type report having a dictionary, but the percentages range from 91 percent among households run by never-married mothers to 98 percent among those with two biological parents present. Similarly, the percentages of youth who report taking extra classes or lessons range from about 18 percent in households headed by fathers (with the biological mother not present) to 34 percent in households with two biological parents.

With regard to the neighborhood quality measures, the average youth in a household headed by a never-married mother reports not hearing gunshots about 6 days a week, whereas those living with two biological parents do not hear them about 6.7 days a week; also, interviewers report less well-kept buildings where the former live, relative to the latter.

Parenting measures tell a similar, though somewhat more mixed, story. For the full sample, youth in households with two biological parents report having supportive mothers (relative to the mean) while those with never-married mothers report the opposite. The mothers perceived as being least supportive are those of youth living with their fathers or others, which is consistent with what one might expect. The association between perceived maternal strictness and household structure is weaker, as never-married mothers are considered the most strict but those previously married (with no spouse currently present) the least strict. These associations correspond to previous research showing that strictness is often used by single parents to manage youth in harsh neighborhood environments (e.g., Furstenberg et al. 1999).

For the full sample, maternal knowledge of youth companions is greatest in two-parent families and lowest among never-married mothers and others (except for those youth living with their fathers). Homes appear best-kept in two-parent families and least-well-kept among never-married mothers, and a similar pattern is observed for the regularity with which meals are eaten together. But the ability of parents to get housework done follows a more mixed pattern.

As for racial differences in these measures, young blacks report fewer computers, less safe neighborhoods, and stricter parenting within each household category, compared to the full sample. Within the black subgroup, for the most part the patterns of association between each measure and household structure are similar to those of the full sample: black youth living with two biological parents are the most likely to have computers and dictionaries, are least likely to hear gunshots, most likely to live where there are well-kept buildings on the street, and most likely to have mothers who are knowledgeable about their companions. For some measures, however, such as taking extra lessons or maternal strictness, strong associations are not apparent.

Overall, the results of Table 4.1 show strong associations between household structure and the human capital enrichments to which young people have access, the home environment and parenting they experience, and the neighborhood environments in which they grow up.

Regression Estimates for Seven Key Outcomes

Table 4.2 shows coefficient estimates on household structure indicators for each of seven outcomes, with two specifications per outcome: Equation (3.2), which controls for maternal characteristics and family

Table 4.1 Means on Household and Parenting Characteristics by Household Structure at Age 12

	Enrichment						Neighborhood			
	In the past month, has your home usually had a computer? (%)		In the past month, has your home usually had a dictionary? (%)		In a typical week, did you spend any time taking extra classes or lessons? (%)		In a typical week, how many days do you *not* hear gunshots in your neighborhood?		How well-kept are the buildings on the street where the youth lives? (mean = 0, var. = 1)	
	Full sample	Blacks	Full sample	Blacks	Full sample	Blacks	Full sample	Blacks	Full sample	Blacks
Total	58.0	35.9	95.8	92.9	28.5	29.3	6.55	6.17	0.11	−0.36
At age 12, sample member lived with:										
Both biological parents	72.1	53.4	98.0	99.3	33.7	28.6	6.65	6.39	0.34	−0.07
Mother, never married	20.9	20.1	91.1	92.9	22.7	28.7	6.05	5.74	−0.51	−0.71
Mother, had been married, no spouse in household	46.0	34.6	94.3	91.4	26.8	28.3	6.59	6.07	−0.13	−0.32
Mother and her spouse	49.6	37.4	93.5	90.1	25.3	29.6	6.48	6.28	−0.01	−0.26
Father	57.4	43.4	95.1	94.8	17.9	27.7	6.43	6.37	−0.09	−0.37
Other	42.1	31.5	93.5	92.3	25.0	34.8	6.41	6.27	−0.07	−0.49
Sample size	4,412	1,185	4,410	1,185	4,392	1,181	4,384	1,166	3,910	1,052

Parenting

	Mother is supportive (mean = 0, var. = 1)		Mother is strict		Mother's knowledge of respondent's companions when she is not home (mean = 0, var. = 1)		How well-kept is the interior of the youth's home? (mean = 0, var. = 1)		Number of days per week housework gets done when it is supposed to?		Number of days per week respondent eats dinner with family?	
	Full sample	Blacks	Full sample	Blacks	Full sample	Blacks	Full sample	Blacks	Full sample	Blacks	Full sample	Blacks
Total	-0.05	-0.13	56.0	63.2	0.01	-0.08	0.05	-0.19	5.63	5.53	5.17	4.53
At age 12, sample member lived with:												
Both biological parents	0.10	-0.06	57.1	63.1	0.12	0.04	0.24	0.08	5.70	5.53	5.33	4.50
Mother, never married	-0.17	-0.19	62.3	65.3	-0.13	-0.16	-0.37	-0.52	5.54	5.64	4.58	4.43
Mother, had been married, no spouse in household	-0.16	-0.11	50.1	63.7	-0.04	0.02	-0.16	-0.14	5.33	5.11	4.86	4.59
Mother and her spouse	-0.13	0.00	54.4	60.6	-0.02	-0.08	-0.05	-0.11	5.71	5.82	5.20	4.56
Father	-0.36[a]	-0.47[a]	61.8[a]	62.0[a]	-0.42[a]	-0.40[a]	-0.31	-0.25	5.58	5.66	5.21	4.39
Other	-0.33[a]	-0.42[a]	53.4[a]	61.9[a]	-0.13[a]	-0.28[a]	-0.03	-0.41	5.70	5.49	5.33	4.84
Sample size	4,259	1,140	4,250	1,138	4,257	1,140	3,811	1,026	4,373	1,163	4,376	1,164

NOTE: Table includes respondents born between 1982 and 1984.

[a] Household structure is measured at age 12, but these youth were asked about these topics in Round 1, when some of them were older. Therefore, some youth were living with their mothers or with mother figures by this time.

SOURCE: Authors' tabulations from NLSY97.

98

Table 4.2 Effects of Household Structure on Outcomes: without and with Neighborhood and Parenting Characteristics

| | Natural log of hourly wage | | | | | | | |
| | Full sample | | Blacks | | Black males | | Black females | |
At age 12, sample member lived with:	(1)	(2)	(1)	(2)	(1)	(2)	(1)	(2)
Mother, never married	0.000	0.002	−0.035	−0.042	−0.099*	−0.117**	0.021	0.027
	(0.028)	(0.028)	(0.044)	(0.047)	(0.056)	(0.055)	(0.071)	(0.076)
Mother, had been married, no spouse in household	0.006	0.008	−0.016	−0.016	−0.056	−0.048	0.017	0.026
	(0.026)	(0.026)	(0.050)	(0.050)	(0.068)	(0.065)	(0.077)	(0.079)
Mother and her spouse	0.036*	0.035	−0.055	−0.054	−0.050	−0.040	−0.056	−0.050
	(0.022)	(0.022)	(0.043)	(0.044)	(0.053)	(0.052)	(0.067)	(0.068)
Father	0.017	0.043	−0.017	0.004	−0.138*	−0.100	0.129	0.116
	(0.050)	(0.055)	(0.077)	(0.088)	(0.081)	(0.083)	(0.141)	(0.179)
Other	0.028	0.026	0.045	0.038	−0.018	−0.047	0.101	0.090
	(0.035)	(0.035)	(0.056)	(0.058)	(0.060)	(0.057)	(0.093)	(0.101)
Enrichment, neighborhood, and parenting variables included	no	yes	no	yes	no	yes	no	yes
Observations	3,604	3,604	904	904	429	429	475	475
R-squared	0.065	0.071	0.073	0.092	0.084	0.159	0.095	0.107

Weeks worked

At age 12, sample member lived with:	Full sample		Blacks		Black males		Black females	
	(1)	(2)	(1)	(2)	(1)	(2)	(1)	(2)
Mother, never married	-1.259	-0.752	-2.454	-1.380	-5.851*	-3.685	-0.015	0.574
	(1.308)	(1.308)	(2.119)	(2.141)	(2.980)	(2.982)	(3.041)	(3.066)
Mother, had been married, no spouse in household	-0.806	-0.408	-3.749*	-2.865	-5.476*	-3.820	-2.172	-1.857
	(1.007)	(1.009)	(2.268)	(2.297)	(3.191)	(3.212)	(3.258)	(3.325)
Mother and her spouse	0.459	0.757	-0.755	0.139	-2.028	-0.614	0.060	1.233
	(0.878)	(0.885)	(2.059)	(2.058)	(2.966)	(3.015)	(2.820)	(2.869)
Father	-0.482	0.366	4.018	4.519	6.110	9.160*	0.102	-2.067
	(1.886)	(2.061)	(3.824)	(4.264)	(4.857)	(5.403)	(5.829)	(6.441)
Other	-3.561**	-3.436**	-2.009	-1.171	-4.378	-2.557	0.467	1.718
	(1.468)	(1.483)	(2.542)	(2.509)	(3.838)	(3.996)	(3.431)	(3.533)
Enrichment, neighborhood, and parenting variables included	no	yes	no	yes	no	yes	no	yes
Observations	4,364	4,364	1,166	1,166	557	557	609	609
R-squared	0.065	0.075	0.073	0.102	0.105	0.156	0.091	0.142

(continued)

100

Table 4.2 (continued)

	High school dropout/GED							
	Full sample		Blacks		Black males		Black females	
	(1)	(2)	(1)	(2)	(1)	(2)	(1)	(2)
At age 12, sample member lived with:								
Mother, never married	0.120***	0.086***	0.094**	0.065	0.109*	0.055	0.088	0.075
	(0.029)	(0.029)	(0.043)	(0.042)	(0.064)	(0.067)	(0.058)	(0.057)
Mother, had been married, no spouse in household	0.090***	0.070***	0.096**	0.083**	0.138**	0.114*	0.043	0.047
	(0.020)	(0.020)	(0.041)	(0.041)	(0.060)	(0.063)	(0.054)	(0.054)
Mother and her spouse	0.076***	0.058***	0.001	-0.011	-0.029	-0.069	0.021	0.018
	(0.018)	(0.017)	(0.035)	(0.034)	(0.053)	(0.054)	(0.045)	(0.046)
Father	0.087**	0.064	0.010	0.028	0.138	0.091	-0.148*	-0.065
	(0.039)	(0.042)	(0.068)	(0.073)	(0.100)	(0.109)	(0.084)	(0.088)
Other	0.084***	0.071**	0.051	0.044	0.066	0.041	0.035	0.023
	(0.031)	(0.030)	(0.053)	(0.052)	(0.081)	(0.082)	(0.067)	(0.064)
Enrichment, neighborhood, and parenting variables included	no	yes	no	yes	no	yes	no	yes
Observations	4,396	4,396	1,186	1,186	568	568	618	618
R-squared	0.153	0.185	0.173	0.213	0.190	0.240	0.193	0.248

Enrolled in 4-year college or not enrolled, bachelor's degree or more

	Full sample		Blacks		Black males		Black females	
	(1)	(2)	(1)	(2)	(1)	(2)	(1)	(2)
At age 12, sample member lived with:								
Mother, never married	-0.128***	-0.089***	-0.094**	-0.067*	-0.098**	-0.063	-0.098	-0.092
	(0.022)	(0.022)	(0.040)	(0.040)	(0.046)	(0.049)	(0.063)	(0.063)
Mother, had been married, no spouse in household	-0.092***	-0.065***	-0.04?	-0.014	-0.073	-0.029	-0.010	-0.006
	(0.021)	(0.020)	(0.044)	(0.044)	(0.053)	(0.055)	(0.071)	(0.071)
Mother and her spouse	-0.131***	-0.110***	-0.078*	-0.067	-0.018	-0.018	-0.128**	-0.119*
	(0.019)	(0.019)	(0.042)	(0.042)	(0.058)	(0.057)	(0.062)	(0.061)
Father	-0.150***	-0.101***	-0.075	-0.058	-0.038	-0.003	-0.178*	-0.156
	(0.033)	(0.036)	(0.069)	(0.075)	(0.092)	(0.098)	(0.105)	(0.115)
Other	-0.106***	-0.085***	-0.062	-0.052	-0.069	-0.061	-0.063	-0.045
	(0.027)	(0.027)	(0.048)	(0.048)	(0.055)	(0.058)	(0.075)	(0.075)
Enrichment, neighborhood, and parenting variables included	no	yes	no	yes	no	yes	no	yes
Observations	4,396	4,396	1,186	1,186	568	568	618	618
R-squared	0.229	0.263	0.162	0.197	0.137	0.192	0.221	0.263

(continued)

Table 4.2 (continued)

	ASVAB							
	Full sample		Blacks		Black males		Black females	
	(1)	(2)	(1)	(2)	(1)	(2)	(1)	(2)
At age 12, sample member lived with:								
Mother, never married	-5.101***	-2.736*	-1.276	0.426	-1.099	1.191	-0.730	0.481
	(1.538)	(1.513)	(2.240)	(2.219)	(3.044)	(3.167)	(3.263)	(3.209)
Mother, had been married, no spouse in household	-2.901**	-1.311	-2.160	-0.473	-2.711	-0.355	-1.480	-1.156
	(1.278)	(1.250)	(2.364)	(2.328)	(3.225)	(3.257)	(3.530)	(3.528)
Mother and her spouse	-3.363***	-2.000*	2.058	3.221	4.360	5.166	-0.032	1.656
	(1.218)	(1.183)	(2.274)	(2.256)	(3.233)	(3.330)	(3.005)	(3.064)
Father	-4.222*	-3.743	1.507	1.859	2.946	3.052	-0.549	1.090
	(2.274)	(2.319)	(3.334)	(3.401)	(4.727)	(4.694)	(5.161)	(5.339)
Other	-5.587***	-4.925***	-0.343	0.479	0.760	1.443	-1.716	-0.622
	(1.826)	(1.856)	(2.664)	(2.667)	(3.682)	(3.849)	(3.863)	(3.675)
Enrichment, neighborhood, and parenting variables included	no	yes	no	yes	no	yes	no	yes
Observations	4,103	4,103	1,072	1,072	543	543	529	529
R-squared	0.349	0.387	0.267	0.304	0.241	0.286	0.310	0.357

103

| | Full sample | | Unmarried with a child | | | | | |
| | | | Blacks | | Black males | | Black females | |
	(1)	(2)	(1)	(2)	(1)	(2)	(1)	(2)
At age 12, sample member lived with:								
Mother, never married	0.125***	0.098***	0.054	0.020	0.119*	0.099	0.005	−0.003
	(0.029)	(0.030)	(0.044)	(0.045)	(0.064)	(0.067)	(0.066)	(0.067)
Mother, had been married, no spouse in household	0.050***	0.036*	0.048	0.022	0.131**	0.098	−0.041	−0.039
	(0.019)	(0.019)	(0.044)	(0.044)	(0.063)	(0.065)	(0.065)	(0.065)
Mother and her spouse	0.065***	0.052***	0.046	0.021	0.050	0.049	0.045	0.021
	(0.017)	(0.017)	(0.043)	(0.043)	(0.058)	(0.061)	(0.063)	(0.064)
Father	0.080**	0.060	0.038	0.025	0.022	0.004	0.134	0.152
	(0.038)	(0.039)	(0.076)	(0.081)	(0.112)	(0.123)	(0.106)	(0.108)
Other	0.085***	0.076**	0.063	0.047	0.154*	0.160*	0.001	−0.012
	(0.029)	(0.030)	(0.052)	(0.054)	(0.084)	(0.086)	(0.072)	(0.073)
Enrichment, neighborhood, and parenting variables included	no	yes	no	yes	no	yes	no	yes
Observations	4,401	4,401	1,184	1,184	566	566	618	618
R-squared	0.136	0.154	0.107	0.130	0.096	0.132	0.144	0.176

(continued)

Table 4.2 (continued)

	Ever incarcerated							
	Full sample		Blacks		Black males		Black females	
	(1)	(2)	(1)	(2)	(1)	(2)	(1)	(2)
At age 12, sample member lived with:								
Mother, never married	0.079***	0.066***	0.084***	0.071***	0.163***	0.140***	0.014	0.016
	(0.018)	(0.018)	(0.024)	(0.024)	(0.044)	(0.044)	(0.021)	(0.021)
Mother, had been married, no spouse in household	0.043***	0.036***	0.052**	0.051**	0.058	0.042	0.054**	0.067***
	(0.012)	(0.012)	(0.023)	(0.023)	(0.036)	(0.037)	(0.026)	(0.027)
Mother and her spouse	0.042***	0.037***	0.036*	0.035*	0.054	0.051	0.020	0.028
	(0.011)	(0.011)	(0.020)	(0.020)	(0.036)	(0.039)	(0.019)	(0.020)
Father	0.004	-0.012	0.039	0.027	0.071	0.061	0.006	-0.018
	(0.019)	(0.021)	(0.041)	(0.043)	(0.065)	(0.073)	(0.026)	(0.035)
Other	0.055***	0.051***	0.053*	0.044	0.096*	0.088	0.016	0.013
	(0.020)	(0.020)	(0.030)	(0.031)	(0.056)	(0.058)	(0.029)	(0.027)
Enrichment, neighborhood, and parenting variables included	no	yes	no	yes	no	yes	no	yes
Observations	4,430	4,430	1,216	1,216	598	598	618	618
R-squared	0.279	0.291	0.352	0.374	0.406	0.435	0.121	0.199

NOTE: The household structure category "two biological parents" was the omitted household structure category in the regression models. Robust standard errors clustered by family are shown in parentheses. Regressions include respondents born between 1982 and 1984. Variables were measured in Round 8 of the NLSY97, from October 2004 to July 2005. Neighborhood, enrichment, and parenting variables are the variables reported in Table 4.1. Control variables include respondent's age at Round 8 interview, mother's age when she had her first child, whether mother is an immigrant, number of siblings in the respondent's household at age 16, mother's educational attainment, mother's hours worked, average family income at ages 14–15, and month of Round 8 interview. Missing data dummies were included for all explanatory variables except for race/gender. Statistical significance is denoted as follows: * $p < 0.10$; ** $p < 0.05$; *** $p < 0.01$.

SOURCE: Authors' tabulations from NLSY97.

income, and Equation (4.1), which adds to Equation (3.2) the 11 household characteristics just described.[8] As in Chapter 3, estimates are presented for the full sample as well as for subsamples of all blacks, black males only, and black females only. Comparing coefficients on a particular household structure across the two specifications within a group indicates how much of the observed relationship between household structure and each outcome can be accounted for by the inclusion of human capital enrichment, parenting, and neighborhood environment characteristics.

Controlling for the set of human capital enrichment, parenting, and neighborhood variables substantially reduces the estimated associations between household structure and many of the seven outcomes. For example, the estimated coefficients on living with a never-married mother are reduced by up to 46 percent (in the model predicting ASVAB percentile). This coefficient in the remaining models is reduced by anywhere from 16 percent (incarceration) to 40 percent (weeks worked). The coefficients on other household structure variables are reduced by smaller but still notable magnitudes.

Yet statistically and substantively significant effects of household structure remain even after controlling for human capital, parenting, and neighborhood characteristics. For example, young adults who lived with a never-married mother are 9 percentage points less likely than those who lived with both biological parents to be enrolled in a four-year college or to have a bachelor's degree in their early twenties, even after controlling for the other variables in the model (including family income). They are 10 percentage points more likely to be unmarried with a child and 7 percentage points more likely to have ever been incarcerated.

The estimated equations for the black subgroup show a similar story. Most of the coefficients on living with a never-married mother are reduced by percentages similar to those for the full sample (for example, by 15 percent in the incarceration model and by 29 percent in the college enrollment/degree model). In the cases just mentioned, the estimated coefficient remained statistically significant. As with the full sample, even though adding the household characteristics reduces the magnitude of the household structure coefficients, some of the remaining effects are substantively significant.[9]

In many cases, the point estimates for the black subgroups (black males only, black females only, or for the two groups combined) are similar in magnitude to those estimated for the full sample. Though fewer of the coefficients in these equations are statistically significant to begin with (due at least partly to the smaller sample sizes on which they are estimated), we generally find that enrichment, parenting, and neighborhood measures account for larger parts of estimated household structure effects for young black males than for young black females. Among young black females, fewer coefficients on household structure are significant to begin with, and the effects on coefficient estimates of adding the additional variables are generally smaller. Notably, the coefficient estimates for living with a never-married mother are greater among black males than among black females in the models predicting wages, weeks worked, being unmarried with a child, and incarceration.

To further assist in understanding the many results presented in Table 4.2, the coefficient estimates are presented graphically for a subset of four outcomes. First, results from regressions predicting the outcome of high school dropout/GED are shown in Figure 4.1, Panel A. Specifically, the figure shows coefficient estimates (expressed in percentage points) for household structures of never-married mothers, and of mothers who had previously been married. Recall that the comparison group is the household structure of both biological parents. The estimates are shown for two specifications (without and then with controls for enrichment, neighborhood, and parenting characteristics) separately for each of four samples (the full sample, blacks, black males, and black females). The same type of information is shown in the remaining panels of Figure 4.1, with Panel B showing estimates from regressions predicting whether the sample member was unmarried with a child, Panel C showing estimates from regressions predicting whether the sample member was ever incarcerated, and Panel D showing estimates from regressions predicting the number of weeks worked.

Overall, the results in Table 4.2 and the Figure 4.1 series indicate that, together, human capital enrichment, parenting, and neighborhood characteristics account for substantial portions of the associations between household structure and the outcomes we examine. But some associations between household structure and outcomes do remain in most cases, even after controlling for these other characteristics.

Because the household structure coefficients are affected by the inclusion of the three sets of household characteristics, it is reasonable to expect that those household characteristics themselves have significant associations with the outcomes examined. Because we are interested primarily in the significance of the conceptual set of variables, Table 4.3 presents p-values for F-tests on the joint significance of coefficients for each of the three sets of measures (three variables for human capital enrichment, six variables for parenting, and two variables for neighborhood environment). Estimates of the individual coefficients and standard errors are reported in Table A.5, found in Appendix A.

The low p-values observed in Table 4.3 indicate that each of the three sets has jointly significant effects on most young adult outcomes we examine. For the full sample, the human capital enrichment and neighborhood measures each are jointly statistically significant in predicting five of the seven outcomes: weeks worked, all three of the educational attainment and achievement outcomes, and being unmarried with a child. The parenting or home environment measures are jointly significant in four models, including all three predicting educational attainment and achievement as well as the model predicting incarceration.

To provide some insight into the results of these joint significance tests, we discuss selected findings from the specific measures, reported in Table A.5. With regard to the human capital enrichment measures, all three—having a computer, having a dictionary, and taking extra classes or lessons—tend to show positive, statistically significant, and substantively important associations with the educational outcomes. For example, with the inclusion of each additional enrichment factor, the average youth has a 3- to 7-percentage-point lower likelihood of being a high school dropout (compared to a mean dropout/GED rate of 16.8 percent for this sample), a 3- to 9-percentage-point greater likelihood of being enrolled in a four-year college or the recipient of a bachelor's degree (compared to a mean of 30.6 percent), and an ASVAB score that is 4.0 to 5.7 percentile points higher (compared to a mean of 51.4).

As for the parenting and home environment measures, we find some evidence that perceptions of mothers as being supportive are correlated with positive outcomes, though the effects tend to be substantively small. For example, a one-standard-deviation increase in the perceived supportiveness of mothers is associated with a 2-percentage-point increase in the probability of being enrolled in a four-year college. Ma-

Figure 4.1 Effects of Household Structure on Outcomes, without and with Enrichment, Neighborhood, and Parenting Controls

Panel A: High school dropout/GED (percentage points)

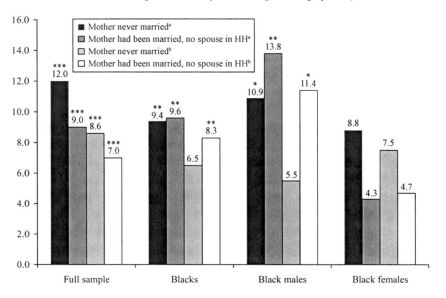

Panel B: Unmarried with a child (percentage points)

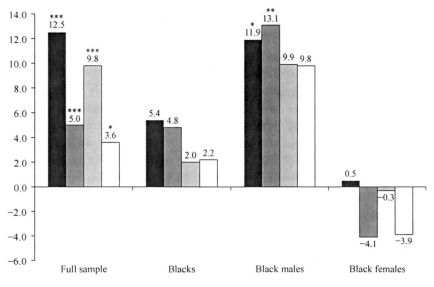

[a] Without controls for enrichment, neighborhood, and parenting.
[b] With controls for enrichment, neighborhood, and parenting.

Figure 4.1 (continued)

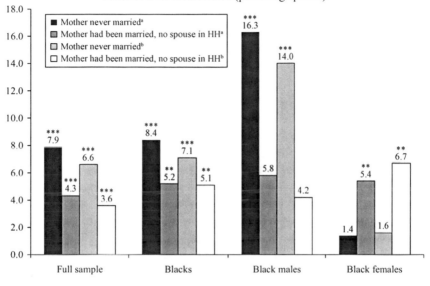

Panel C: Ever incarcerated (percentage points)

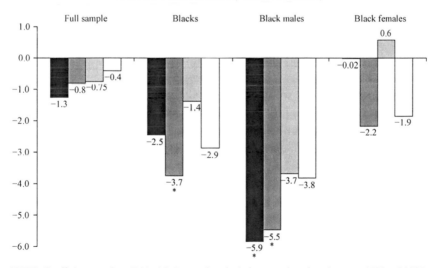

Panel D: Weeks worked (number of weeks)

NOTE: Coefficients are from Table 4.2. Regressions include respondents born between 1982 and 1984. Regression variables were measured in Round 8 of the NLSY97, from October 2004 to July 2005. Neighborhood, enrichment, and parenting variables are the variables reported in Table 4.1. Control variables include respondent's age at Round 8 interview, mother's age when she had her first child, whether mother is an immigrant, number of siblings in the respondent's household at age 16, mother's educational attainment, mother's hours worked, average family income at ages 14–15, and month of Round 8 interview. Missing data dummies were included for all explanatory variables except for race/gender. Statistical significance is denoted as follows: * $p < 0.10$; ** $p < 0.05$; *** $p < 0.01$.

[a] Without controls for enrichment, neighborhood, and parenting.

[b] With controls for enrichment, neighborhood, and parenting.

ternal knowledge of the youth's companions tends to be associated positively with educational outcomes (with relatively small substantive effects) and negatively with incarceration (with moderate substantive effects). Homes with well-kept interiors tend to be positively associated with educational achievement and negatively associated with incarceration. For example, getting housework done is associated positively with measures of education while eating dinner together is negatively associated with incarceration (though the estimated effects are substantively small and not always statistically significant).

Finally, with regard to the neighborhood variables, both the perceived absence of gunshots, reported by the respondent, and the impression of well-kept buildings, reported by the interviewer, are significantly associated with educational outcomes and with some risky or illegal activities, though substantively these effects are small.[10]

The discussion above focuses on results for the full sample. With regard to results for the black subgroups (black males, black females, or both together), Table 4.3 indicates that the associations between human capital enrichment or neighborhood characteristics and the seven outcomes are less often significant than in the full sample; this is due to sample size limitations.

However, the parenting and home environment measures are jointly significant in most equations for outcomes among the three subgroups, just as they are for the full sample. More specifically (see Table A.5), maternal knowledge of youth companions is often a significant predictor, especially in the equation for incarceration; the estimated effects are of similar or slightly smaller magnitudes than those of the full sample. Having a well-kept interior and getting housework done are positively related to college attendance and scoring well on the ASVAB.

In comparing black males and females, we see that the parenting variables have significant effects on outcomes more frequently for young black men than for young black women. For young black men, the parenting and home environment measures are statistically significant in equations for weeks worked, being a high school dropout or attending college, ASVAB scores, and incarceration. Maternal knowledge of companions is often significantly related to outcomes, especially for dropping out of high school (a 1-standard-deviation increase is associated with a 5-percentage-point lower likelihood of dropping out).

These results suggest that home environments and parental behaviors might importantly affect the propensity of young black men to fail in and disconnect from school. Why these factors affect black males more than black females or other youth remains unclear. Perhaps the young men are more hurt by the absence of positive role models in fathers, or perhaps their behavioral responses are more negative when there is a lack of adequate supervision or structure in the home. More research is undoubtedly needed to understand these effects more fully. But, at a minimum, the apparently greater sensitivity of outcomes for young black men to these measures of the home environment is important to consider when discussing potential remedies, as we do in Chapter 5.

Can we make any causal inferences about these correlates of household structure and their estimated effects on behavior? As noted earlier in the chapter, the human capital enrichment and neighborhood characteristics are likely influenced by family income, though we control for this in our regressions. Characteristics of parenting and the home environment may be more directly a function of household structure.

We also do not necessarily attribute causality to any of the estimated relationships between outcomes and the household characteristics. For example, whether computer use really contributes to human capital and labor market productivity has been questioned by DiNardo and Pischke (1997) in their well-known response to Krueger (1993). Whether estimates of "neighborhood effects" truly reflect causal impacts has long been questioned (e.g., Jencks and Mayer 1990), while even the effects of taking extra classes or lessons are subject to multiple interpretations. For instance, taking classes might simply mean that young people are more likely to be supervised by adults for some time period. If the classes are remedial in nature, they might also reflect weaker underlying academic skills of the student, and this might tend to offset any positive effects of taking extra classes that might otherwise be observed.

Furthermore, the estimated associations likely also reflect endogenous relationships. For instance, in those cases where supportive mothers are positively associated with various outcomes, the successful youth might be more inclined to view their parents in a positive light when they are successful than when they are not. On the other hand, the growing interest in how a variety of noncognitive skills affect educational and employment outcomes (as reflected in the work of James

Table 4.3 Joint Significance of Human Capital Enrichment, Parenting, and Neighborhood Characteristics on Outcomes

Set of variables for which F-test was conducted	Natural log of hourly wage	Weeks worked	High school dropout/GED	Enrolled in 4-year college or not enrolled, bachelor's degree or more	ASVAB	Unmarried with a child	Ever incarcerated
			Full sample				
Human capital enrichment variables	0.598	0.028**	0.000***	0.000***	0.000***	0.000***	0.348
Parenting variables	0.324	0.723	0.000***	0.000***	0.000***	0.319	0.000***
Neighborhood variables	0.544	0.030**	0.000***	0.000***	0.000***	0.001***	0.167
Observations	3,604	4,364	4,396	4,396	4,103	4,401	4,430
R-squared	0.071	0.075	0.185	0.263	0.387	0.154	0.291
			Blacks				
Human capital enrichment variables	0.519	0.187	0.026**	0.169	0.030**	0.214	0.481
Parenting variables	0.744	0.086*	0.001***	0.000***	0.000***	0.569	0.026**
Neighborhood variables	0.313	0.370	0.455	0.001***	0.181	0.020**	0.781
Observations	904	1,166	1,186	1,186	1,072	1,184	1,216
R-squared	0.092	0.102	0.213	0.197	0.304	0.130	0.374

	Black males						
Human capital enrichment variables	0.601	0.791	0.115	0.012**	0.101	0.612	0.520
Parenting variables	0.306	0.062*	0.043**	0.052*	0.091*	0.593	0.080*
Neighborhood variables	0.236	0.057**	0.504	0.008***	0.098*	0.020**	0.500
Observations	429	557	568	543	566	598	
R-squared	0.159	0.156	0.240	0.192	0.286	0.132	0.435
	Black females						
Human capital enrichment variables	0.857	0.090*	0.235	0.810	0.167	0.460	0.999
Parenting variables	0.854	0.780	0.016**	0.002***	0.006***	0.212	0.407
Neighborhood variables	0.645	0.560	0.951	0.048**	0.935	0.389	0.007***
Observations	475	609	618	618	529	618	618
R-squared	0.107	0.142	0.248	0.263	0.357	0.176	0.199

NOTE: Cells show p-values for F-tests of whether coefficients on variables in each indicated set were jointly equal to zero. Regressions from Specification 4.1, whose household structure coefficients were reported in Table 4.2. The point estimates and standard errors for each measure in each category are shown in Table A.5. The sample includes respondents born between 1982 and 1984. Variables were measured in Round 8 of the NLSY97, from October 2004 to July 2005. Neighborhood, enrichment, and parenting variables are the variables reported in Table 4.1. Control variables include respondent's age at Round 8 interview, mother's age when she had her first child, whether mother is an immigrant, number of siblings in the respondent's household at age 16, mother's educational attainment, mother's hours worked, average family income at ages 14–15, and month of Round 8 interview. Missing data dummies were included for all explanatory variables except for race/gender. Statistical significance is denoted as follows: * $p < 0.10$; ** $p < 0.05$; *** $p < 0.01$.

SOURCE: Authors' tabulations from NLSY97.

Heckman and others) is certainly consistent with many of our findings, especially regarding parenting effects.

Despite these caveats, we are inclined to believe that some portion of the associations we estimate between household characteristics and outcomes is causal (though we cannot say how much). The observed patterns of explanation are consistent with expectations: human capital enrichment variables are more likely to affect educational outcomes, whereas parental monitoring and structure in the home have an influence not only on education but also on ever being incarcerated. Furthermore, the estimated differences across demographic groups are consistent with expectations: given the much greater propensity of young black men to disengage from school than young black women, the risky behaviors of young black males are more sensitive to environmental and parental effects than those of young black females. Finally, the estimates tend to be robust across multiple educational or behavioral outcomes and across a variety of demographic groups. The overall groups of human capital enrichment, neighborhood, and parental/home environment variables are each likely to be more reliable and less susceptible to unobserved heterogeneity than are the component variables within each category.[11] The relative robustness of the individual coefficient estimates to the various specifications we have tried also suggests that some of these effects might be real as well.[12]

At the same time, we acknowledge that our ability to fully account for the observed effects of household structure remains limited in many cases, and that the explanatory power of many groups of these variables in our estimated equations is not high.

CONCLUSION

In this chapter we present descriptive statistics on eleven measures of household characteristics. These measures—encompassing constructs of human capital enrichment, neighborhood quality, and parenting/home environment—are likely correlated both with household structure and with seven different outcomes of young adulthood in the areas of employment, education, and risky behaviors. We estimate regression equations showing the extent to which controlling for these characteristics can account for the estimated relationships between household structure and each of the outcomes, and we also consider the effects of the household characteristics themselves on the outcomes.

Our results suggest the following:

- Human capital enrichment (as measured by the presence of computers or dictionaries and attendance at extra lessons or classes) and neighborhood safety are strongly associated with household structure, and they are especially lacking in households headed by never-married mothers.

- Parenting measures of maternal supportiveness and strictness, maternal knowledge of youths' companions, orderliness of the home and timeliness of housework, and eating dinner together are also associated with household structure, as single parents have less orderly houses and know less about their children's companions.

- Human capital enrichment, parenting, and neighborhood characteristics account for significant portions (generally 15-40 percent) of the estimated effects of household structure on youth outcomes, controlling for family income and a number of maternal characteristics.

- Even after controlling for these additional measures, statistically and substantively significant effects of household structure remain for a number of outcomes.

- Enrichment, neighborhood, and parenting measures themselves have significant effects on youth educational and behavioral outcomes.

- Estimated effects of household characteristics on outcomes for blacks are similar to those for the full sample, while those estimated for black males are somewhat stronger than those for black females.

These findings have mixed implications for our understanding of how household structure affects outcomes observed among youth. On the one hand, the correlations between household structure and enrichment/neighborhood effects likely are largely spurious (except for those operating through parental income, for which we have controlled) and do not represent causal effects of family structure. On the other hand, the fact that several parenting variables have significant effects on educational and behavioral outcomes—and that the residual effects of household structure after controlling for all these factors remain fairly important—suggest some important causal effects of household structure as well.

These findings also have very mixed implications for the future well-being of low-income youth growing up in single-parent families. Youth growing up in single-parent households have less access to enrichment materials or activities (at least as measured here) and are frequently located in less safe neighborhoods than their counterparts from two-parent families. At least on the dimensions measured here, these youth face challenges in achieving academic success and avoiding risky behaviors.

The results of this chapter suggest that a number of correlates of more successful outcomes, however, can be managed by parents and perhaps enhanced through appropriate policy interventions. These predictors seem to operate either through household structure or independently of it. Providing more human capital enrichment in the home or in school, improving neighborhood safety, and improving parental supportiveness and supervision of youth might all improve the opportunities that young people have and thus contribute to their greater success in terms of educational attainment and the labor market.

We consider these implications in greater detail in the concluding chapter.

Notes

1. See BLS (2006) for a description of the general categories of such variables and their availability in different rounds.
2. The bivariate correlations among these three measures ranged from 0.05 to 0.14.
3. The bivariate correlations among these measures ranged from 0.02 to 0.37, with most being 0.13 or less.
4. The correlation between these two measures was 0.20.
5. Sample members were asked the number of days a week, on average, that they *did* hear gunshots. So that higher values will indicate more positive neighborhood environments, we subtract the responses from 7.
6. Sample weights are used in the summary statistics, but not in the regression analyses.
7. The unweighted values of variables noted above were standardized to have a mean

of 0 and a variance of 1. The weighted descriptive statistics shown in Table 4.1 do not have a mean of 0.

8. In Chapter 3, the seven outcomes were analyzed for all NLSY97 sample members. In the current chapter, these outcomes are analyzed for the subgroup of sample members who were born in 1982–1984. Thus, the estimates for Specification 3.2 shown in Table 4.1 may be different from those reported in Chapter 3.

9. For example, blacks who lived with never-married mothers are 7 percentage points less likely to attend a four-year college, and 7 percentage points more likely to be incarcerated, compared to blacks who lived with both biological parents.

10. For example, each additional day that gunshots are not heard is associated with a reduction in the probability of dropping out of high school or being unmarried with a child by 1 to 2 percentage points, and it increases the probability of being enrolled in a four-year college by 1 percentage point. A 1-standard-deviation increase in the degree to which buildings on the street are well-kept is associated with a decrease in the probability of dropping out of 3 percentage points and an increase in the probability of four-year college enrollment of 2 percentage points.

11. This assumes that the unobserved characteristics that are correlated with the individual variables in each group are not all the same and may tend to offset each other.

12. More information is available from the authors on specifications in which these variables have been entered separately or in various combinations.

5

Conclusion

Gaps in employment and education outcomes between young African Americans and whites have persisted over the past several decades, despite significant strides. Along some dimensions, such as employment and especially incarceration among young men, the racial gaps have even widened.

Why do these gaps persist? One hypothesis suggests that the increasing tendency of young blacks to grow up in female-headed households during the past few decades has contributed to the persistent and even growing racial gaps in outcomes. While the trends in household structure might themselves reflect other causes of worsening employment opportunities and outcomes among black men, these trends might also contribute to a worsening set of outcomes among the next generation of youth.

In particular, young people growing up in single-parent families on average have fewer financial resources, more stress, less supervision, and fewer male role models than their counterparts who grow up with both biological parents; thus, the widespread incidence of female headship in black families might well contribute to less successful outcomes for black youth.

Yet despite a substantial empirical literature on family structure and its effects on youth outcomes, relatively little evidence to date exists on how family structure affects a wide variety of outcomes among black youth as compared with others, and for males versus females within racial groups. Moreover, evidence on the mechanisms and pathways through which these effects might occur has been somewhat limited.

In this book, we have used data from the NLSY—and especially the 1997 cohort—to explore these issues. We focus on a set of outcomes for young people that include employment, school enrollment and attainment, cognitive achievement, and participation in various risky or illegal behaviors (such as bearing children outside marriage or committing a crime and becoming incarcerated). We estimate the statistical relationships between these outcomes and the structure of households in which youth grow up, controlling for a number of individual youth and maternal characteristics.

We measure household structure—primarily at age 12—in a way that captures some of the history of that structure as well as its current status. We measure six categories of household structure, comparing 1) youth living with both of their biological parents (our reference group) to those living with 2) never-married mothers, 3) previously married mothers who now have no spouse in the household (i.e., those divorced or separated), 4) mothers who have been previously married but have a new spouse (i.e., are remarried), 5) biological fathers but not their mothers, and 6) others (including grandparents, adoptive parents, foster parents, or other arrangements). We present some evidence on the stability of these arrangements over time, which motivates our decision to focus on household structure and its history as of age 12, an age that generally captures household structure during childhood as well as the adolescent and teen years for most young people.

We include estimates of the effects of household structure on these outcomes for youth, both without and with controls included for family income, which is the most obvious mechanism through which such effects might operate. We also estimate these equations separately for blacks, and for black males and black females, to examine whether household structure has different effects across these groups. We consider the effects of household structure on race and gender differences in each outcome, to infer the extent to which differences in household structure can account for persisting racial gaps.

Of course, any estimated effects might not be truly causal, and instead might reflect a range of other variables (like the family backgrounds of the mothers themselves) that are correlated both with household structure and with outcomes but not measured in our data. We do, however, include many control variables to mitigate concerns about omitted variable bias; these include maternal employment, maternal education, maternal age at first birth, immigrant status, and the sample member's age and number of siblings. To further address concerns about the identification of causal effects, we also estimate a series of fixed-effects models in which we measure the effects of differences in household structure on differences in outcomes, either between siblings or over time for the same sample member.

After estimating the models that include controls for sample member characteristics, maternal characteristics, and family income, we add variables to the models to measure some of the mechanisms or pathways through which household structure might affect youth outcomes. These include a set of variables measuring human capital enrichment in the home (the presence of computers or dictionaries as well as extra courses or classes taken); another set measuring neighborhood environment, especially safety; and a third set measuring parental behavior and home environment, including the degree of parental monitoring of friends, the regularity with which work gets done or dinners are eaten together, and the youth's perception of parental strictness or supportiveness.

We consider the extent to which these measures account for observed effects of household structure on youth and young adult outcomes, and whether they themselves have significant effects—among the full sample, separately for blacks, and separately for black males and black females.

The remainder of this chapter summarizes our results and their implications for further research and for policy.

SUMMARY OF EMPIRICAL FINDINGS

We begin in Chapter 2 by presenting data on the employment, educational, and behavioral outcomes of youth, separately by race and gender, and looking at how at least some of these outcomes have evolved over time. We compare data for similarly aged youth at comparable points in the business cycle in the 1980s and 2000s.

We find, as expected, that educational and employment outcomes continue to be lower for blacks and Hispanics than for whites. Young women have generally made more progress in both education and employment than have young men in all racial groups over the past two decades, and women now finish high school and enroll in college at higher rates than men within each racial group.

But young black men, in particular, are falling even further behind whites and Hispanics in a number of dimensions, and substantially behind black women on measures of educational attainment and achievement. The greater participation of young blacks in risky behaviors—especially having children outside of marriage and (among men) engaging in crime and becoming incarcerated—is noteworthy as well. For all groups, but especially for young blacks, dropping out of high school is associated with fewer weeks worked and a range of risky behaviors, including crime and incarceration.

In Chapter 3, we turn our attention to the structures of households in which youth live at age 12, and how these structures affect a range of youth outcomes. We find, as expected, that young blacks are much more likely to grow up in families without both biological parents than are young whites. Indeed, the frequency of growing up without both parents in the home is about 50 percent among youth overall and about 80 percent among young blacks. Family incomes of those growing up without both biological parents are much lower than those with both parents, especially among youth living with never-married mothers. But other personal characteristics, such as maternal education, are highly correlated with household structure as well, suggesting a variety of possible reasons (both causal and noncausal) for why outcomes of youth in single-parent households might lag behind those of their counterparts.

When we examine the statistical relationships between household structure and young adult outcomes, we find that these structures are modestly related to labor market outcomes but more substantially related to youths' educational attainment and achievement as well as to nonmarital childbearing and incarceration. Controlling for household income accounts for some—generally about a fourth to a half—of these estimated effects, but by no means all of them.

Estimated effects are generally just as large among young blacks as young whites, and often appear even larger among young black men than young black women—especially on outcomes like weeks worked and incarceration (though small sample sizes limit the statistical significance of the estimated differences in most cases). Indeed, differences in household structure seem to account for more than a third of the higher black male rate of incarceration (relative to white males), more than half of black males' greater tendency to drop out of high school, and most of their differences in college attendance in these equations. Absent the changes in household structure over time, the rates at which blacks drop out of high school would be several percentage points lower than for whites (while their college attendance would be correspondingly higher); the same is true of their tendencies to have children outside of marriage and to become incarcerated. A set of fixed-effects models, both between siblings and over time for the same individuals, also shows some significant effects of household structure on outcomes, suggesting at least partly causal effects of the former on the latter.

In Chapter 4, we seek to establish more of the mechanisms and pathways (besides household income) through which the effects of household structure on outcomes might work. We find that measures of human capital enrichment and neighborhood safety are highly correlated with family structure, in that the highest rates of enrichment and safety are observed among those living with both biological parents and the lowest among those living with never-married mothers. Parenting behaviors are also somewhat correlated with household structure, as single mothers are perceived by youth as being stricter, monitoring youth behaviors and peers less closely, and getting housework done and having dinner together less frequently.

The data also show that human capital enrichment, neighborhood safety, and parenting behaviors account for fairly substantial portions (15 to 40 percent) of the estimated effects of household structure on youth outcomes. All three sets of variables have jointly significant estimated effects on youth outcomes, with the human capital measures having somewhat stronger effects on education and the neighborhood and parenting measures mattering a bit more for behavioral outcomes. Again, estimated effects for young black men are as strong as or stronger than those for young black women or for whites and Hispanics.

To what extent are all of these estimated effects on youth outcomes—including those for household structure as well as those for the mediating variables—truly causal, rather than just reflecting omitted variables that we cannot measure? Regarding the estimated effects of household structure, we note that the maternal characteristics for which we control (including employment, education, age, nativity, and number of children) are more extensive than those included in many other studies. Furthermore, our fixed-effects estimates, both across siblings and over time for the same individual, also suggest that some parts of the estimated household effects are causal, even though these tests have some major practical limitations that likely cause them to understate the effects of changes in household structure on outcomes.

Whether or not the estimated effects of human capital enrichment, neighborhood environment, and parenting variables themselves are also causal is harder to establish. Nevertheless, these estimates are quite robust across many different outcomes and different race or gender groups among young adults. The particular pattern of estimated effects—a pattern of human capital variables affecting education outcomes strongly while neighborhood and parenting variables affect nonmarital births and incarceration relatively more—is consistent with a causal interpretation. And considering the sets of variables as constructs of interest (instead of interpreting each variable separately) also likely strengthens the interpretation of the construct as a whole as being causal and weakens the likelihood that the sets of variables are fully driven by their correlations with omitted factors, as we note in Chapter 4.

Summing Up

In all, our analysis suggests that black youth—and especially young black males—continue to lag behind whites (and Hispanics as well) quite dramatically on educational, employment, and behavior outcomes, and in some cases (such as employment and incarceration) they are falling even further behind. Almost certainly, the fact that so many of these young people grow up in families without both biological parents—and especially with never-married mothers—has impeded progress along many dimensions and contributed to worsening outcomes in some cases. All else being equal, the high incidence of single parenthood in the black community has limited the incomes of the households in which young people grow up, and also the ability of parents to provide stable and orderly environments in which they can monitor the activities of their youth and guide them appropriately.

And the apparently larger effects of single-parent households on some outcomes of young black males than on those of young black females suggests the particularly important role that household structure might play in generating poor employment and behavioral outcomes for this group. We can only speculate about exactly why this is true. Behavioral issues during adolescence and the teen years for young males in general seem more serious than those for young females, especially in low-income families, and a gender gap in academic performance and achievement has now appeared among all groups.

But, especially among lower-income black families and neighborhoods, the effects of household structure seem to matter more for males.

Perhaps this reflects the impact of a lack of positive male role models and mentors for this group, or the lack of strong paternal supervision on their behavior. Alternatively, the interactions between single mothers and their sons might be more strained than between mothers and their daughters. Positive impacts of programmatic treatments for young girls but not boys have been seen in other contexts as well, such as the Moving to Opportunity experiments (though the effects of New Hope employment assistance were stronger for boys). Whatever their causes, the particularly negative impacts on outcomes of young black males are noteworthy and require further attention by researchers and policymakers.

At the same time, however, it is also clear that household structure does not fully account for the continuing racial gaps in most of these outcomes. For instance, racial gaps in employment, childbearing outside marriage, and incarceration between black (male) youth and others persist even after controlling for single parenthood. Furthermore, the disadvantages caused by single parenthood are compounded by the lower education levels and earnings of these parents, the lack of cognitive enrichment in their homes, and their residence in less safe neighborhoods—all of which do not appear to be caused by single parenthood per se.

In sum, many young blacks and especially black males are swimming against the tide as they grow up: they face a multitude of disadvantages associated with (causally or otherwise) coming of age in single-parent families that limit their opportunities in life. These disadvantages reflect a wide range of factors in the home, and are then compounded by various neighborhood effects, presumably in school and out of it. Accordingly, the analysis here implies that a wide array of policy responses is necessary to offset the full range of disadvantages these young people face as they grow up. Identifying policies that can offset these many disadvantages in cost-effective ways is the challenge that we now must address.

IMPLICATIONS FOR FURTHER RESEARCH

Our analysis strategy has involved the estimation of regression models that include an extensive set of controls and the estimation of fixed-effects models (both for siblings and for individuals over time). In some cases, these strategies eliminate the effects of household structure (for example, in the cases of wages and hours worked). But for other outcomes, effects of household structures on outcomes remain (for example, in the cases of educational attainment, being unmarried with a child, or ever having been incarcerated). Such persistent effects of household structure in these cases lead us to conclude cautiously that the effects of household structure that we estimate are at least partly causal. Our fixed-effects estimates tend to reinforce this view.

Yet the estimation strategies that we use cannot convincingly eliminate the possibility that omitted factors that are correlated both with household structure and with these outcomes are actually driving some of these results. Thus, we cannot claim definitively that our estimated effects of household structure are truly causal. A first implication for further research is thus to pursue additional estimation strategies that can identify causal effects of household structure on the types of outcomes we examine in this study. These might include instrumental variables or other variants of the fixed-effects models estimated here.

In Chapter 4, we show estimates of the effects of sets of human capital enrichment, neighborhood safety, and parenting/home environment characteristics on seven outcomes. These effects are estimated from models with an extensive set of controls. While the estimates of these variables seem somewhat robust across different samples, and while our results are consistent with what one might expect (for example, as with the human capital enrichment variables related to educational outcomes and with the parenting variables related to risky behavior outcomes), claims about causality are weaker here than for household structure and require even more attention.

A second implication for further research, then, is the need for identifying the causal effects of the types of enrichment, neighborhood, and parenting variables that we examine in this paper. More broadly, developing a fuller understanding of the mechanisms through which household structure might affect youth outcomes, and also of the family and neighborhood factors that might tend to offset these effects, remains a high priority for research. Better understanding of the timing of these effects and of how they vary across different household structures (including families with stepparents and cohabiting adults), is in order as well. And understanding more about the role of noncustodial fathers, and the impact of their relationships with youth on outcomes, is important too.

Research that addresses causality and robustness will provide further confidence for policy prescriptions like the ones offered below, which are designed to influence household structure and its correlates and to improve outcomes for all young adults, but especially for young minorities.

POLICY IMPLICATIONS

Overall, it seems that the goals of public policy with respect to the household structures in which young people grow up should be two-fold: first, to reduce the frequency of young people growing up with single parents; and, second, to improve opportunities and outcomes for young people who continue to live in such homes.

Given those goals, what might such a set of policies include? To what extent should we target the behaviors and outcomes of single parents versus those of their children and youth? And how much effort should be placed on the prevention of single parenthood through broad improvements in opportunity for young people, as opposed to efforts to offset its negative effects once it has occurred?

Broadly, our evidence implies the need for the following set of five policy efforts:

1) *Discouraging single parenthood*—by promoting marriage or discouraging unwed pregnancy, whenever possible;

2) *Raising the incomes of unmarried working parents*—either by improving their earnings capacity or by further supplementing their low earnings in a variety of ways;

3) *Improving the schooling and neighborhood environments of youth*—to offset early disadvantages and prevent them from worsening over time;

4) *Improving supervision of youth and parenting*—in programs and at home, both among custodial and noncustodial parents; and

5) *Limiting racial disparities in employment and crime/incarceration among youth more generally*—through a wide range of general programmatic and policy efforts.

But do we know how to accomplish these goals cost-effectively? Our evidence of what works and what doesn't in each area is limited. Absent such clear evidence, we need a comprehensive effort that generates continuing research and evaluation in each area, while we experiment with a broad range of programmatic and policy efforts in the meantime. We briefly discuss some possible options, and what we know and don't know about their cost-effectiveness, for each policy goal below.

1) Discouraging Single Parenthood

Marriage promotion received attention as a policy priority for the Bush administration, particularly through its Healthy Marriage Initiative. Some evidence exists that there are approaches that successfully promote marriage among middle-class couples, but virtually no evidence is available pointing to what, if anything, works for promoting healthy marriages among the poor (Dion 2005; Ooms 2007). Perhaps such information will emerge from the current round of demonstration projects funded by the U.S. Department of Health and Human Services in this area. We remain somewhat skeptical that enough is known about how to influence the marital choices of low-income young people. We also doubt that the kinds of interventions used in these efforts (like counseling) are sufficient to overcome the huge barriers to marital matching and success that such young people face, especially in the form of low employment and earnings capacities, and the stresses on marriage that these constraints generate.

Furthermore, among families where the children have the same never-married mother but each has a different biological father, the exact candidate for marriage to the mother is unclear, and some offspring will no doubt become stepchildren of these new fathers, which is a much more ambiguous outcome from the children's point of view (Acs 2006). Promotion of marriage before such circumstances develop would likely be more successful than afterwards, if at all possible.

While the cost-effectiveness of various marriage promotion options remains quite uncertain, we have a somewhat greater understanding of how to deter (or at least delay) childbearing among those who are un-married, especially teens. While any one option in this area, such as abstinence-only, is unlikely to be effective, strategies that combine mul-tiple approaches of education, community service activities, messages through the news media, and youth development appear somewhat more successful (National Campaign to Prevent Teen and Unplanned Pregnancy 2008).

There is also some evidence to date that improved enforcement of child support obligations on noncustodial fathers tends to discourage unwed pregnancy (Pirog and Ziol-Guest 2006). On the other hand, cer-tain aspects of current child-support enforcement efforts appear to have some negative unintended consequences on the employment and par-enting of poor noncustodial fathers.

Finally, perhaps the most effective strategies to further marriage and prevent unwed pregnancy would involve improving the earnings and employment prospects of young African American men, as we dis-cuss more fully below.

2) Raising Incomes among Unmarried Working Poor Adults

Because lower family income accounts for at least some part of the negative effects of single parenthood on youth outcomes, raising the family incomes of working single parents might be another way of offsetting these negative effects. While virtually no one advocates the resurrection of welfare policies that simply provide cash income main-tenance to the poor (without being tied to work), further supplementing the incomes of working-poor adults might be helpful. Indeed, evidence from a variety of experimental efforts that supplemented the earnings of low-income welfare mothers shows that earnings supplements for low-income parents can raise achievement among children and youth (Morris, Gennetian, and Duncan 2005).

The Earned Income Tax Credit (EITC) is the most obvious vehicle for expanding the incomes of the working poor. The current federal credit, which is worth approximately $4,800 at its peak for low-income working parents with two or more children, clearly encourages greater work effort while providing more income to the poor (Meyer and Rosen-baum 2001). A number of states also supplement the federal EITC with their own tax credits.

But the federal EITC and state credits might be amended in a number of ways. For one thing, the current phaseout rate (at 21 percent of earnings above roughly $16,000 for families with two children) might discourage work among two-parent families or discourage marriage, as both tend to raise family income and therefore reduce eligibility for the EITC. Reducing the phaseout rate, raising the threshold at which phaseout begins, or counting only parts of a spouse's earnings in calculating household income would provide more income to these families while reducing taxes on both work and marriage. Greater cash payments to those with three or more children, or to those with just one child, might well be considered too.

And, given the poor wages and employment incentives for low-income young men (especially those who are noncustodial fathers), an expansion of the EITC—either to childless adults in general or to noncustodial fathers in particular (for those who are at least keeping up with their current child support orders)—might be justifiable. Indeed, the State of New York has recently undertaken the latter approach, whereas several analysts have advocated some version of the former (Berlin 2007; Edelman, Holzer, and Offner 2006).[1]

And there are a number of other ways of supplementing the earnings of the working poor that might also be particularly helpful to children and youth in these families. Specifically, policies that extend paid parental and medical leave to low-income working parents, as well as child care and health insurance, are likely to relieve stress and generate gains for youth in these families (Waldfogel 2007).

In addition, a variety of approaches that would raise the earnings capacity of working poor adults need to be explored and more rigorously evaluated. A lengthy literature already exists on the cost-effectiveness of job training for disadvantaged youth and adults, which mostly shows the modest effectiveness of modest programs for adults. But newer approaches have been developed in recent years that involve some combination of 1) education or training, usually at community colleges, perhaps targeted at growing sectors of the economy (like health care, construction, and the like) that provide above-minimal wages to non-college workers; 2) a range of work supports, including child care assistance and transportation as well as stipends for any training period; and 3) job placement efforts that seek to match these workers with better employers and jobs. These efforts would all be coordinated by labor market intermediaries—third-party groups (such as community-based organizations or other for-profit or nonprofit associations) that bring together workers, employers, training providers, and public supports.[2]

Indeed, one recent proposal (Holzer 2007) calls for the federal government to fund competitive grants to states and local areas for building such "advancement systems." States would be required to carefully measure performance while more rigorous evaluation evidence on these approaches was generated, and renewal of these grants over time would depend on states incorporating any knowledge that was generated from these performance measures and from evaluation.

Finally, efforts that directly try to raise wages on the demand side of the labor market for low-income workers might be included here as well (Bartik 2001; Holzer 2007). These would include occasional increases in the minimum wage (or indexing it to inflation), legal efforts to make it easier for low-wage workers to unionize, and local economic development efforts (like tax credits and grants) that particularly reward the generation of higher-wage jobs. The potential effects of higher minimum wages and unionism on employment rates must, of course, be considered in any such efforts.

3) Improving Schooling Options and Neighborhood Safety for Poor Youth

Since the negative effects of single parenthood on youth seem clearest for academic outcomes, such as completing high school and enrolling in college, and since these effects operate through (or are compounded by) weak academic enrichment opportunities in the home and residence in unsafe neighborhoods, policies might be undertaken to directly combat these problems by providing for more academic opportunities and improving neighborhood quality for low-income and minority young people, especially in single-parent families.

Of course, exactly how to accomplish these worthy goals can be (and frequently is) heavily debated elsewhere. The returns to high-quality early childhood education efforts, despite their high cost, have been quite well established (Ludwig and Sawhill 2007), and the returns to universal prekindergarten programs in Oklahoma and elsewhere look especially strong for lower-income students and minorities (Gormley and Gayer 2005). But large questions remain about whether the strongest programs (like the Carolina Abecedarian Project and the High/ Scope Perry Preschool Program) can be replicated and scaled up, and whether these effects tend to fade with time. The cost-effectiveness of many other approaches in the K-8 years—such as smaller class sizes, school choice efforts, and high-stakes testing—are even less clear. Efforts to improve teacher quality in poor areas (Bendor, Bordoff, and Furman 2007) are less controversial and could have important effects on educational quality for poor children. Desegregation of schools might also tend to limit racial gaps in student achievement (Card and Rothstein 2005; Weiner, Lutz, and Ludwig 2006), but these efforts are much more politically controversial, and their legal status has been cast into doubt by recent court rulings.[3]

But as low-income youth enter their high school years in any location, it is desirable that they should face a better range of pathways to success in postsecondary education, employment, or both. Some of these pathways could be based on high-quality Career and Technical Education (CTE) along with early labor market activity; indeed, we have fairly strong evidence on the cost-effectiveness of Career Academies and Tech Prep in improving postschool employment outcomes for at-risk youth (Lerman 2007). Others involve improving access to higher education through better financial aid and other supports, as in Project Opening Doors, which has generated some positive results in recent evaluations (Brock and Richburg-Hayes 2006). Some proposals would improve Pell grant availability and reduce the complexity of the application process (Dynarski and Scott-Clayton 2007). Direct efforts to reduce the very high dropout rates that characterize high schools in many poor urban and rural areas must also be pursued, even while efforts to evaluate what works in this area continue (Pennington 2006).

How might we improve the quality of neighborhoods in which low-income and minority young people grow up? Turner, Popkin, and Rawlings (2008) review what we know about legal and programmatic efforts to improve housing or neighborhood quality among poor minorities and to reduce residential segregation. The Moving to Opportunity (MTO) experiments seem to have mixed effects, which are generally more positive for female than male youth (Kling, Ludwig, and Katz 2005). And we know fairly little about the cost-effectiveness of efforts to improve home environments by supporting greater asset development, particularly home ownership, among the poor (McKernan and Ratcliffe 2007).

Other efforts to improve services to youth at the community level, such as the Youth Opportunity grants recently distributed by the U.S. Department of Labor or the Harlem Children's Zone, seem promising (Edelman, Holzer, and Offner 2006) but also require more rigorous evaluation. These, of course, are specific approaches within the broader category of "youth development" programs at the community level that might well decrease a variety of negative behaviors and outcomes among youth and improve their education and earnings outcomes over time (Eccles and Gootman 2002).

4) Improving Supervision of Youth and Parenting

To the extent that low-income single parenthood may result in less positive parenting and home environments (perhaps associated with the greater instability and stresses that are prevalent in many such homes), greater provision of child care or after-school care as well as direct parenting supports might be helpful.

While some analysts (e.g., Besharov and Samari 2001) argue that the provision of child care for low-income working parents is already ample, this view is disputed elsewhere (e.g., Greenberg, Ewen, and Matthews 2006). The need to improve the *quality* of such care seems less controversial, though exactly how to do so remains open to question (Blau 2001). Improving access to center-based care (as well as early childhood education) seems to be one route to improving child care quality.

Also, youth supervision might be improved through the kinds of positive youth development efforts cited above, including programs like Boys and Girls Clubs of America, and also through a variety of after-school programs, such as those supported by the 21st Century Community and Learning Centers. While the evaluation evidence on the latter efforts has been somewhat disappointing to date (James-Burdumy et al. 2005), efforts to identify cost-effective strategies in this area should continue.

Is it possible to directly improve parenting by other means, such as interventions for children that include their parents as well? Head Start attempts to do so (Schumacher 2003), though whether it is successful

is open to debate. Other efforts to directly involve parents and improve
their skills at rearing children and youth have appeared in a variety
of contexts, such as the Comer School Development Program (Comer
2004) and the Infant Health and Development Program (Brooks-Gunn,
Liaw, and Klebanov 1992). Indeed, rigorous evaluations have found the
latter to be successful.

In terms of improving parenting, additional efforts could focus on
encouraging noncustodial fathers to have more active and responsible
involvement with their children. Previous research has suggested important potential benefits in this approach (Billingsley 1992; Clayton,
Mincy, and Blankenhorn 2003; Mincy 1994).[4] Indeed, effective fatherhood programs might be considered complementary with, rather than
substitutes for, marriage promotion programs (Ooms et al. 2006).

But what is needed to encourage more effective fatherhood? At
a minimum, it would seem that improving employment opportunities
for noncustodial fathers would be a critical component of any such approach. Among low-income noncustodial fathers, employment rates
and earnings levels are extremely low (Mincy and Sorensen 1998), suggesting perhaps limited earnings capacity with which to support noncustodial children. At the same time, for those who are in arrears on
child support payments (particularly those who have been incarcerated),
the incentive to accept low-wage employment is very low, because the
implicit tax rates on these earnings are so high (up to 50 percent), and
much of the money collected is not even passed through to families
(Holzer, Offner, and Sorensen 2005).

Thus, improving employment among low-income noncustodial fathers might require some reforms in the child support system, along with
employment and training assistance for those with limited employment
options on their own (Bloom and Butler 2007; Edelman, Holzer, and
Offner 2006). Counseling and peer support groups for absent fathers
are also frequently included in such efforts. With respect to the cost-
effectiveness of these programs, the rigorous evaluation of the Parents'
Fair Share program (Miller and Knox 2001) found that the fatherhood
efforts contained in that program modestly improved the quality of parenting among noncustodial fathers but not their employment rates or
child support payments. A more effective approach might require more
rigorously enforced child support payments as well as more generously
supported transitional employment opportunities and additional subsi-

dies, as were provided in the New Hope demonstration in Milwaukee (Duncan, Huston, and Weisner 2007; Primus 2006).

Finally, because so many low-income noncustodial fathers also have criminal records—especially among African Americans—efforts to raise their employment level must address the particular barriers faced by this group. These barriers are substantial on both the demand side of the labor market (employer attitudes and hiring behaviors may discriminate against those with criminal records) and the supply side (the potential workers may lack the requisite skills), as discussed by Holzer (2009). Rigorous evidence on cost-effective approaches here, too, is limited.[5] But in addition to funding successful reentry programs, reducing the legal barriers to employment among those with criminal records might be important as well (Holzer, Raphael, and Stoll 2003).

5) Limiting Racial Disparities in Employment and Crime/ Incarceration among Youth

The evidence presented in this book shows that, even after accounting for differences in household structure, racial gaps remain in some outcomes between whites and blacks, especially among young men. The most striking gaps—in employment levels and incarceration—are partly, but not fully, accounted for by racial gaps in education and basic skills. These discouraging outcomes in turn likely contribute to high rates of single parenthood in the black community, as fewer men are considered worthy prospects for marriage by their potential mates, and fewer are themselves interested in marriage or parenting, given their circumstances.

We have reviewed a variety of efforts above that would ultimately improve the employment prospects of young black men. Some would work through early schooling and employment activities, while others would target working poor adults or hard-to-employ noncustodial fathers and exoffenders. As we also noted above, broad-based efforts to improve opportunities for youth should seek to reduce racial segregation in schools and neighborhoods. Additionally, they should target the labor market discrimination that still exists toward black men of all ages (Holzer 2006; Pager 2007), either through improved enforcement of Equal Employment Opportunity (EEO) laws or better dissemination of information on applicant quality.[6]

Promising employment programs for minority out-of-school youth, such as YouthBuild or the Youth Service and Conservation Corps, could be funded at much greater levels than they are currently (Edelman, Holzer, and Offner 2006), even while efforts continued, through rigorous evaluation, to determine exactly what approach is most cost-effective. At the same time, community-based efforts to combat the alienation and resentments of youth which find their expression in an "oppositional culture" (Mead 2006) could also gain more support. And as a society we might rely less heavily on incarcerating young men for nonviolent drug offenses, as we did in the past (Raphael and Stoll 2007).

Given the enormous social costs associated with the status quo (Holzer et al. 2007), a wide variety of efforts to combat low employment and high incarceration for this population are clearly justified—even if they require some significant expenditure of resources, and even if our knowledge of their cost-effectiveness remains imperfect.

Notes

1. Berlin's (2007) proposal would provide tax credits to low-earning adults regardless of their family income, in order to avoid marriage penalties, while Edelman, Holzer, and Offner (2006) call for more limited payments that would still depend on family income. To avoid large marriage penalties, the latter propose to only count half of a second earner's income when computing eligibility. Berlin's proposal would likely cost more than $30 billion a year, while Edelman, Holzer, and Offner estimate that theirs would cost about $10 billion.

2. The training models for working poor adults that target the demand side of the labor market more clearly include sectoral training, tax credits for incumbent worker training, and building career ladders, either within smaller establishments (like nursing homes) or across them. See Holzer and Martinson (2005) and Osterman (2007).

3. In particular, the U.S. Supreme Court struck down voluntary school desegregation efforts in Seattle and Louisville in rulings delivered on June 28, 2007. Justice Anthony Kennedy, who was the swing vote in each of these 5-4 rulings, has indicated he may support certain desegregation efforts that do not target individual students by race.

4. Our own tabulations from the NLSY97 (not reported here) also document the very limited involvement of never-married fathers with their noncustodial children relative to fathers in every other group. These, too, suggest some important potential benefits to improving fathering practices among this group.

5. Preliminary results from MDRC's evaluation of the Center for Employment Opportunities (or CEO) in New York suggest major reductions in recidivism from efforts to provide services and transitional jobs to ex-offenders right after release from prison, though impacts on employment beyond the program were disappointing.

6. In particular, labor market intermediaries might be able to reduce statistical discrimination in hiring by providing employers with information about job applicants that the employers themselves might not find. For evidence on how information from background checks can actually reduce discrimination against black men, see Holzer, Raphael, and Stoll (2006).

Appendix A
Background Tables

Table A.1 Recursive Employment and Education Regressions for Black Males

	Natural log of hourly wage, past year			Weeks worked, past year			High school dropout, Nov. 2004		
	Model 1	Model 2	Model 3	Model 1	Model 2	Model 3	Model 1	Model 2	Model 3
Age	0.050***	0.045***	0.044***	1.639***	1.269***	1.402***	0.003	0.003	−0.003
	(0.011)	(0.011)	(0.011)	(0.483)	(0.489)	(0.493)	(0.011)	(0.009)	(0.009)
Education level[a]									
Not enrolled, high school dropout or GED		−0.201***	−0.165**		−15.434***	−12.701***			
		(0.073)	(0.076)		(3.419)	(3.541)			
Not enrolled, high school degree		−0.074	−0.056		−8.291***	−7.222**			
		(0.069)	(0.072)		(3.156)	(3.224)			
Not enrolled, some college or associate's degree		−0.039	−0.017		−1.914	−0.964			
		(0.070)	(0.072)		(3.003)	(3.109)			
Enrolled, two-year college		−0.176**	−0.157**		−7.881**	−7.110*			
		(0.074)	(0.075)		(3.963)	(4.102)			
Enrolled, four-year college		−0.145*	−0.137*		−10.364***	−9.643***			
		(0.081)	(0.083)		(3.446)	(3.515)			
GPA in high school		−0.038	−0.048		0.160	−0.106		−0.228***	−0.177***
		(0.032)	(0.033)		(1.312)	(1.319)		(0.024)	(0.025)
ASVAB percentile		0.045**	0.054***		0.966	1.111		−0.115***	−0.090***
		(0.019)	(0.020)		(1.012)	(1.021)		(0.018)	(0.018)
Unmarried and has children			0.026			1.367			0.102***
			(0.036)			(1.596)			(0.033)
Risky behaviors prior to age 18									
Drank alcohol			−0.002			−1.965			−0.044
			(0.033)			(1.551)			(0.028)

	(1)	(2)	(3)	(4)	(5)	(6)	(7)	(8)	(9)
Smoked cigarettes			-0.037 (0.035)			2.001 (1.525)			0.080*** (0.029)
Smoked marijuana			-0.023 (0.033)			-2.372 (1.687)			0.038 (0.033)
Ever stole something worth $50 or more, joined a gang, attacked someone, or was arrested			-0.021 (0.033)			-1.576 (1.583)			0.061** (0.027)
Ever incarcerated			-0.031 (0.048)			-6.593*** (2.165)			0.222*** (0.047)
Constant	1.009*** (0.287)	1.312*** (0.325)	1.356*** (0.344)	-5.181 (15.856)	18.685 (17.726)	22.525 (18.209)	0.530 (0.322)	0.650** (0.308)	0.468 (0.298)
Observations	679	679	679	910	910	910	923	923	923
R-squared	0.051	0.093	0.106	0.025	0.097	0.127	0.029	0.247	0.324

NOTE: Robust standard errors are shown in parentheses. Variables were measured in Round 8 of the NLSY97, from October 2004 to July 2005. Dummy variables controlling for month of interview are included but not reported. Missing data dummies were included for all explanatory variables except for race/gender. Statistical significance is denoted $p < 0.10$, $p < 0.05$, and $p < 0.01$.
[a] The omitted educational category in the regression is "not enrolled, some college or college degree."

Table A.2 Recursive Employment and Education Regressions for Black Females

	Natural log of hourly wage, past year			Weeks worked, past year			High school dropout, Nov. 2004		
	Model 1	Model 2	Model 3	Model 1	Model 2	Model 3	Model 1	Model 2	Model 3
Age	0.067***	0.058***	0.060***	1.528***	1.144***	1.174***	-0.015*	-0.012*	-0.015***
	(0.010)	(0.011)	(0.011)	(0.427)	(0.437)	(0.443)	(0.008)	(0.008)	(0.007)
Education level[a]									
Not enrolled, high school dropout or GED		-0.320***	-0.297***		-14.749***	-12.892***			
		(0.078)	(0.081)		(2.834)	(3.009)			
Not enrolled, high school degree		-0.264***	-0.256***		-7.828***	-7.246***			
		(0.068)	(0.071)		(2.317)	(2.411)			
Not enrolled, some college or associate's degree		-0.220***	-0.211***		-5.076**	-4.803**			
		(0.068)	(0.071)		(2.232)	(2.300)			
Enrolled, two-year college		-0.266***	-0.259***		-6.592**	-5.873**			
		(0.081)	(0.084)		(2.777)	(2.868)			
Enrolled, four-year college		-0.271***	-0.273***		-6.687***	-6.740***			
		(0.074)	(0.076)		(2.311)	(2.323)			
GPA in high school		-0.068**	-0.062**		1.905*	1.718		-0.181***	-0.143***
		(0.030)	(0.031)		(1.154)	(1.169)		(0.021)	(0.022)
ASVAB percentile		0.114***	0.105***		2.489***	2.468***		-0.090***	-0.082***
		(0.021)	(0.022)		(0.899)	(0.925)		(0.016)	(0.016)
Unmarried and has children			-0.044			-0.905			0.061***
			(0.031)			(1.353)			(0.023)
Risky behaviors prior to age 18									
Drank alcohol			0.009			-0.263			-0.029
			(0.032)			(1.419)			(0.025)

	(1)	(2)	(3)	(4)	(5)	(6)	(7)	(8)	(9)
Smoked cigarettes			-0.002			-0.636			0.103***
			(0.031)			(1.462)			(0.026)
Smoked marijuana			0.044			1.490			0.063**
			(0.034)			(1.566)			(0.029)
Ever stole something worth $50 or more, joined a gang, attacked someone, or was arrested			0.015			-2.545*			0.042*
			(0.029)			(1.303)			(0.022)
Ever incarcerated			-0.165*			-7.309*			0.295***
			(0.096)			(3.935)			(0.075)
Constant	0.472	1.068***	0.938***	15.320	26.010**	35.927***	0.701***	0.858***	0.693***
	(0.297)	(0.341)	(0.356)	(10.246)	(11.907)	(12.618)	(0.259)	(0.246)	(0.236)
Observations	814	814	814	1,031	1,031	1,031	1,041	1,041	1,041
R-squared	0.068	0.137	0.151	0.027	0.113	0.127	0.022	0.252	0.318

NOTE: Robust standard errors are shown in parentheses. Variables were measured in Round 8 of the NLSY97, from October 2004 to July 2005. Dummy variables controlling for month of interview are included but not reported. Missing data dummies were included for all explanatory variables except for race/gender. Statistical significance is denoted $p < 0.10$, ** $p < 0.05$, and *** $p < 0.01$.

[a] The omitted educational category in the regression is "not enrolled, some college or college degree."

Table A.3 Household Structure Stability of Respondents between Ages 2 and 12 (%)

At age 2, sample member lived with:	Both biological parents	Mother, never married	Mother, had been married, no spouse in household	Mother and her spouse	Father	Other	Total	Sample size
At age 12, sample member lived with:								
Both biological parents	98.13	0.00	0.24	0.48	1.15	1.30	51.42	3,535
Mother, never married	0.01	95.34	0.00	0.00	0.00	0.59	5.62	653
Mother, had been married, no spouse in household	0.01	0.00	42.66	42.78	1.29	2.41	14.75	1,139
Mother and her spouse	0.08	0.00	52.59	52.56	1.46	5.91	18.28	1,394
Father	0.13	0.11	0.93	2.05	92.93	2.63	4.62	341
Other	1.64	4.55	3.57	2.12	3.18	87.16	5.32	479
Total	100	100	100	100	100	100	100	7,541
Sample size	3,583	679	845	1,794	314	326	7,541	

NOTE: Proportions are calculated from the NLSY97 cohort using Round 8 sample weights.

Table A.4 Household Structure Stability of Respondents between Ages 12 and 16

At age 12, sample member lived with:	Both biological parents	Mother, no other parent	Mother and her spouse	Father	Other	Total	Sample size
At age 16, sample member lived with:							
Both biological parents	94.86	3.54	18.30	13.16	7.52	53.65	3,629
Mother, no other parent	2.74	74.13	33.34	8.39	13.50	23.60	1,996
Mother and her spouse	0.43	13.72	40.14	10.43	15.15	11.64	823
Father	1.07	3.73	4.38	61.56	16.40	5.94	422
Other	0.89	4.88	3.85	6.45	47.44	5.17	490
Total	100	100	100	100	100	100	7,360
Sample size	3,425	1,741	1,352	341	501	7,360	

NOTE: proportions are calculated from the NLSY97 cohort using round 8 sample weights. Measure of household structure at age 16 combines "mother, never married" and "mother, had been married, no spouse in hh" categor es into "mother, no other parent."

Table A.5 Effects of Neighborhood and Parenting Characteristics on Outcomes, with Household Structure at Age 12

	Full sample						
	Natural log of hourly wage	Weeks worked	High school dropout/GED	Enrolled in 4-year college or not enrolled, bachelor's degree or more	ASVAB	Unmarried with a child	Ever incarcerated
Enrichment variables							
In the past month, has your home usually had a computer?	0.009 (0.017)	0.240 (0.676)	−0.059*** (0.013)	0.086*** (0.014)	5.650*** (0.925)	−0.061*** (0.013)	−0.012 (0.008)
In the past month, has your home usually had a dictionary?	0.038 (0.033)	3.181** (1.448)	−0.066** (0.032)	0.033* (0.018)	3.994** (1.659)	−0.061* (0.031)	0.003 (0.018)
In a typical week, did you spend any time taking extra classes or lessons?	−0.008 (0.017)	1.310** (0.656)	−0.034*** (0.012)	0.057*** (0.015)	5.586*** (0.857)	−0.015 (0.012)	−0.007 (0.007)
Neighborhood variables							
In a typical week, how many days do you *not* hear gunshots in your neighborhood?	−0.003 (0.006)	0.347 (0.238)	−0.017*** (0.005)	0.013*** (0.003)	1.273*** (0.292)	−0.016*** (0.005)	−0.004 (0.003)
How well kept are the buildings on the street where the youth lives?	−0.009 (0.010)	0.864** (0.425)	−0.026*** (0.009)	0.021*** (0.008)	1.110** (0.524)	−0.013 (0.009)	−0.005 (0.005)

	(1)	(2)	(3)	(4)	(5)	(6)	(7)
Parenting variables							
Mother is supportive	−0.012*	−0.112	−0.002	0.019***	0.258	−0.003	−0.001
	(0.007)	(0.303)	(0.006)	(0.006)	(0.375)	(0.006)	(0.003)
Mother is strict	0.009	0.144	−0.004	0.016	0.398	−0.003	0.003
	(0.015)	(0.599)	(0.011)	(0.012)	(0.745)	(0.011)	(0.007)
Mother's knowledge of respondent's companions when she is not home	−0.001	0.377	−0.032***	0.017***	0.844**	−0.011	−0.016***
	(0.008)	(0.325)	(0.007)	(0.006)	(0.383)	(0.007)	(0.004)
How well kept is the interior of the youth's home?	0.015	0.027	−0.008	0.024***	1.089**	−0.011	−0.012**
	(0.009)	(0.419)	(0.009)	(0.007)	(0.522)	(0.008)	(0.006)
Number of days per week housework gets done when it is supposed to?	−0.002	0.239	−0.007**	0.012***	1.286***	0.001	−0.002
	(0.004)	(0.173)	(0.003)	(0.003)	(0.205)	(0.003)	(0.002)
Number of days per week respondent eats dinner with family?	0.004	−0.079	−0.001	−0.003	−0.176	−0.002	−0.002
	(0.003)	(0.141)	(0.003)	(0.003)	(0.179)	(0.003)	(0.002)
Observations	3,604	4,364	4,396	4,396	4,103	4,401	4,430
R-squared	0.071	0.075	0.185	0.263	0.387	0.154	0.291

(continued)

Table A.5 (continued)

	Blacks						
	Natural log of hourly wage	Weeks worked	High school dropout/GED	Enrolled in 4-year college or not enrolled, bachelor's degree or more	ASVAB	Unmarried with a child	Ever incarcerated
Enrichment variables							
In the past month, has your home usually had a computer?	0.019 (0.030)	1.210 (1.398)	-0.053** (0.025)	0.042 (0.026)	2.075 (1.576)	-0.041 (0.030)	0.025 (0.016)
In the past month, has your home usually had a dictionary?	0.025 (0.054)	3.906 (2.534)	-0.072 (0.054)	0.024 (0.028)	4.245* (2.171)	-0.091 (0.057)	0.002 (0.032)
In a typical week, did you spend any time taking extra classes or lessons?	0.033 (0.031)	1.558 (1.337)	-0.032 (0.024)	0.028 (0.025)	2.388* (1.445)	-0.002 (0.030)	-0.004 (0.016)
Neighborhood variables							
In a typical week, how many days do you *not* hear gunshots in your neighborhood?	-0.008 (0.010)	0.113 (0.380)	-0.010 (0.008)	0.018*** (0.005)	0.662 (0.447)	-0.023*** (0.009)	0.000 (0.004)
How well-kept are the buildings on the street where the youth lives?	-0.019 (0.017)	1.019 (0.757)	-0.004 (0.015)	0.012 (0.013)	0.804 (0.831)	-0.006 (0.016)	-0.006 (0.009)

149

Parenting variables

	(1)	(2)	(3)	(4)	(5)	(6)	(7)
Mother is supportive	-0.018	0.054	-0.013	0.003	0.176	-0.003	0.004
	(0.013)	(0.610)	(0.013)	(0.009)	(0.563)	(0.013)	(0.007)
Mother is strict	0.002	3.162**	-0.005	0.044**	2.116	-0.013	-0.007
	(0.027)	(1.274)	(0.025)	(0.022)	(1.326)	(0.028)	(0.015)
Mother's knowledge of respondent's companions when she is not home	0.01	1.112*	-0.039***	-0.001	1.107*	-0.012	-0.021***
	(0.013)	(0.592)	(0.012)	(0.010)	(0.575)	(0.013)	(0.007)
How well kept is the interior of the youth's home?	0.007	0.376	0.000	0.027**	2.055**	-0.020	-0.022**
	(0.017)	(0.847)	(0.016)	(0.013)	(0.838)	(0.018)	(0.010)
Number of days per week housework gets done when it is supposed to?	0.005	0.016	-0.002	0.020***	0.887***	0.007	-0.004
	(0.007)	(0.334)	(0.007)	(0.005)	(0.304)	(0.007)	(0.004)
Number of days per week respondent eats dinner with family?	-0.007	-0.012	-0.010*	-0.005	-0.080	-0.008	0.001
	(0.006)	(0.262)	(0.005)	(0.005)	(0.270)	(0.006)	(0.003)
Observations	904	1,166	1,186	1,186	1,072	1,184	1,216
R-squared	0.092	0.102	0.213	0.197	0.304	0.130	0.374

(continued)

Table A.5 (continued)

	Black males						
	Natural log of hourly wage	Weeks worked	High school dropout/GED	Enrolled in 4-year college or not enrolled, bachelor's degree or more	ASVAB	Unmarried with a child	Ever incarcerated
Enrichment variables							
In the past month, has your home usually had a computer?	0.001 (0.043)	0.775 (2.159)	−0.070* (0.040)	0.085** (0.036)	1.214 (2.170)	−0.016 (0.042)	0.044 (0.030)
In the past month, has your home usually had a dictionary?	0.040 (0.083)	1.605 (3.254)	−0.104 (0.073)	0.036 (0.029)	5.615** (2.529)	−0.088 (0.070)	0.017 (0.047)
In a typical week, did you spend any time taking extra classes or lessons?	0.053 (0.044)	1.467 (2.007)	−0.007 (0.040)	0.054 (0.035)	1.677 (2.053)	0.000 (0.043)	−0.009 (0.029)
Neighborhood variables							
In a typical week, how many days do you *not* hear gunshots in your neighborhood?	−0.018 (0.013)	0.505 (0.520)	−0.013 (0.012)	0.017*** (0.007)	0.936* (0.528)	−0.029** (0.012)	−0.008 (0.008)
How well-kept are the buildings on the street where the youth lives?	−0.016 (0.025)	2.278** (1.099)	−0.005 (0.022)	0.025 (0.017)	1.311 (1.189)	−0.016 (0.022)	−0.005 (0.016)

Parenting variables							
Mother is supportive	−0.037	0.038	0.000	0.000	−0.287	0.025	0.013
	(0.023)	(1.023)	(0.021)	(0.013)	(0.886)	(0.021)	(0.013)
Mother is strict	0.005	5.340***	−0.013	0.002	−0.143	0.045	0.011
	(0.037)	(1.963)	(0.038)	(0.030)	(1.899)	(0.039)	(0.028)
Mother's knowledge of respondent's companions when she is not home	0.036**	1.358	−0.049***	−0.005	1.541*	0.003	−0.028**
	(0.018)	(0.862)	(0.018)	(0.013)	(0.803)	(0.019)	(0.012)
How well kept is the interior of the youth's home?	0.008	−0.260	0.009	0.010	1.121	−0.014	−0.040**
	(0.023)	(1.146)	(0.023)	(0.016)	(1.075)	(0.024)	(0.017)
Number of days per week housework gets done when it is supposed to?	0.008	−0.526	0.017	0.019***	0.815*	0.000	−0.003
	(0.011)	(0.520)	(0.011)	(0.007)	(0.490)	(0.010)	(0.008)
Number of days per week respondent eats dinner with family?	−0.010	0.459	−0.017**	0.000	0.167	−0.011	0.002
	(0.009)	(0.415)	(0.008)	(0.006)	(0.373)	(0.008)	(0.006)
Observations	429	557	568	568	543	566	598
R-squared	0.159	0.156	0.240	0.192	0.286	0.132	0.435

(continued)

Table A.5 (continued)

	Black females						
	Natural log of hourly wage	Weeks worked	High school dropout/GED	Enrolled in 4-year college or not enrolled, bachelor's degree or more	ASVAB	Unmarried with a child	Ever incarcerated
Enrichment variables							
In the past month, has your home usually had a computer?	0.028 (0.045)	2.060 (1.841)	-0.028 (0.032)	-0.030 (0.039)	2.630 (2.393)	-0.037 (0.045)	-0.002 (0.015)
In the past month, has your home usually had a dictionary?	0.020 (0.066)	6.963 (4.285)	-0.001 (0.084)	0.035 (0.052)	4.257 (3.768)	-0.125 (0.096)	-0.004 (0.045)
In a typical week, did you spend any time taking extra classes or lessons?	0.019 (0.045)	2.503 (1.820)	-0.054* (0.032)	0.000 (0.035)	2.957 (2.076)	-0.014 (0.041)	0.001 (0.015)
Neighborhood variables							
In a typical week, how many days do you not hear gunshots in your neighborhood?	0.001 (0.015)	-0.542 (0.569)	-0.002 (0.011)	0.020** (0.008)	0.146 (0.799)	-0.019 (0.013)	0.011*** (0.004)
How well-kept are the buildings on the street where the youth lives?	-0.022 (0.024)	-0.424 (1.094)	0.006 (0.020)	-0.002 (0.020)	0.338 (1.152)	0.003 (0.024)	0.001 (0.009)

Parenting variables

Mother is supportive	-0.011	-0.146	-0.017	-0.004	-0.030	-0.012	0.000
	(0.017)	(0.772)	(0.015)	(0.013)	(0.767)	(0.018)	(0.008)
Mother is strict	-0.009	0.652	0.008	0.086***	4.445**	-0.057	-0.022
	(0.040)	(1.740)	(0.033)	(0.033)	(1.871)	(0.040)	(0.015)
Mother's knowledge of respondent's companions when she is not home	-0.019	0.706	-0.028*	0.002	1.019	-0.030	-0.010
	(0.021)	(0.862)	(0.016)	(0.015)	(0.891)	(0.020)	(0.008)
How well kept is the interior of the youth's home?	0.003	1.103	-0.019	0.044*	2.832**	-0.027	-0.009
	(0.028)	(1.211)	(0.021)	(0.023)	(1.373)	(0.026)	(0.009)
Number of days per week housework gets done when it is supposed to?	0.002	0.421	-0.015*	0.020***	0.817*	0.014	-0.005
	(0.010)	(0.453)	(0.009)	(0.007)	(0.420)	(0.010)	(0.005)
Number of days per week respondent eats dinner with family?	-0.005	-0.342	-0.006	-0.009	-0.244	-0.005	0.001
	(0.008)	(0.359)	(0.007)	(0.007)	(0.385)	(0.008)	(0.002)
Observations	475	609	618	618	529	618	618
R-squared	0.107	0.142	0.248	0.263	0.357	0.176	0.199

NOTE: Robust standard errors clustered by family are shown in parentheses. Regressions include respondents born between 1982–1984. Variables measured in Round 8 of the NLSY97, from October 2004 to July 2005. Neighborhood, enrichment, and parenting variables are the variables reported in Table 4.1. Control variables including respondent's age at Round 8 interview, mother's age when she had her first child, whether mother is an immigrant, number of siblings in the respondent's household at age 16, mother's educational attainment, mother's hours worked, average family income at ages 14–15, and month of Round 8 interview. Missing data dummies were included for all explanatory variables except for race/gender. Statistical significance is denoted: * $p < 0.10$, ** $p < 0.05$, and *** $p < 0.01$.

References

Abe, Yasuyo. 2001. "Changes in Gender and Racial Gaps in Adolescent Anti-social Behavior: The NLSY97 versus the NLSY79." In *Social Awakening: Adolescent Behavior as Adulthood Approaches*, Robert T. Michael, ed. New York: Russell Sage Foundation, pp. 339–378.

Abraham, Katharine. 2003. "Towards a Cost-of-Living Index: Progress and Prospects." *Journal of Economic Perspectives* 17(1): 45–58.

Acs, Gregory. 2006. "Can We Promote Child Well-Being by Promoting Marriage?" *Journal of Marriage and Family* 69(5): 1326–1344.

Acs, Gregory, and Sandi Nelson. 2003. *Changes in Family Structure and Child Well-Being: Evidence from the 2002 National Survey of America's Families.* Washington, DC: Urban Institute.

Altonji, Joseph G., and Charles R. Pierret. 2001. "Employer Learning and Statistical Discrimination." *Quarterly Journal of Economics* 116(1): 313–350.

Amato, Paul R. 2005. "The Impact of Family Formation Change on the Cognitive, Social, and Emotional Well-Being of the Next Generation." *Future of Children* 15(2): 75–96.

Ananat, Elizabeth O., and Guy Michaels. 2008. "The Effect of Marital Break-up on the Income Distribution of Women with Children." *Journal of Human Resources* 43(3): 611–629.

Ashcraft, Adam, and Kevin Lang, 2006. "The Consequences of Teenage Child-bearing." NBER Working Paper 12485. Cambridge, MA: National Bureau of Economic Research.

Aughinbaugh, Alison Aileen, Charles R. Pierret, and Donna S. Rothstein. 2005. "The Impact of Family Structure Transitions on Youth Achievement: Evidence from the Children of the NLSY79." *Demography* 42(3): 447–468.

Barber, Brian K., and Joseph A. Olsen. 1997. "Socialization in Context: Connection, Regulation, and Autonomy in the Family, School, and Neighborhood, and with Peers." *Journal of Adolescent Research* 12(2): 287–315.

Bartik, Timothy J. 2001. *Jobs for the Poor: Can Labor Demand Policies Help?* New York: Russell Sage Foundation.

Bedard, Kelly, and Olivier Deschênes. 2005. "Sex Preferences, Marital Dissolution, and the Economic Status of Women." *Journal of Human Resources* 40(2): 411–434.

Beltran, Daniel O., Kuntal K. Das, and Robert W. Fairlie. 2006. "Do Home Computers Improve Educational Outcomes? Evidence from Matched Current Population Surveys and the National Longitudinal Survey of Youth 1997." IZA Discussion Paper No. 1912. Bonn, Germany: Institute for the Study of Labor.

Bendor, Joshua, Jason Bordoff, and Jason Furman. 2007. "An Education Strategy to Promote Opportunity, Prosperity, and Growth." Hamilton Project strategy paper. Washington, DC: Brookings Institution.

Berlin, Gordon L. 2007. "Rewarding the Work of Individuals: A Counterintuitive Approach to Reducing Poverty and Strengthening Families." *Future of Children* 17(2): 17–42.

Besharov, Douglas J., and Nazanin Samari. 2001. "Child Care after Welfare Reform." In *The New World of Welfare*, Rebecca M. Blank and Ron Haskins, eds. Washington, DC: Brookings Institution, pp. 461–481.

Billingsley, Andrew. 1992. *Climbing Jacob's Ladder: The Enduring Legacy of African-American Families*. New York: Simon and Schuster.

Blank, Rebecca M. 2002. "Evaluating Welfare Reform in the United States." *Journal of Economic Literature* 40(4): 1105–1166.

Blau, David M. 2001. *The Child Care Problem: An Economic Analysis*. New York: Russell Sage Foundation.

Blau, Francine D., and Lawrence M. Kahn. 1997. "Swimming Upstream: Trends in the Gender Wage Differential in the 1980s." *Journal of Labor Economics* 15(1): 1–42.

Blau, Francine D., Lawrence M. Kahn, and Jane Waldfogel. 2000. "Understanding Young Women's Marriage Decisions: The Role of Labor and Marriage Market Conditions." *Industrial and Labor Relations Review* 53(4): 624–647.

Blinder, Alan S., and Janet L. Yellen. 2001. *The Fabulous Decade: Macroeconomic Lessons from the 1990s*. New York: Century Foundation.

Bloom, Dan, and David Butler. 2007. "Overcoming Employment Barriers: Strategies to Help the 'Hard to Employ.'" In *Reshaping the American Workforce in a Changing Economy*, Harry J. Holzer and Demetra Smith Nightingale, eds. Washington, DC: Urban Institute, pp. 155–179.

Bound, John. 1986. "NBER-Mathematica Survey of Inner-City Black Youth: An Analysis of the Undercount of Older Youths." In *The Black Youth Employment Crisis*, Richard B. Freeman and Harry J. Holzer, eds. Chicago: University of Chicago Press, pp. 443–460.

Bradley, Robert H., Bettye M. Caldwell, and Stephen L. Rock. 1988. "Home Environment and School Performance: A Ten-Year Follow-Up and Examination of Three Models of Environmental Action." *Child Development* 59(4): 852–867.

Brock, Thomas, and Lashawn Richburg-Hayes. 2006. *Paying for Persistence: Early Results of a Louisiana Scholarship Program for Low-Income Parents Attending Community College*. New York: MDRC.

Bronars, Stephen G., and Jeff Grogger. 1994. "The Economic Consequences of

Unwed Motherhood: Using Twin Births as a Natural Experiment." *American Economic Review* 84(5): 1141–1156.

Brooks-Gunn, Jeanne, Fong-ruey Liaw, and Pamela Kato Klebanov. 1992. "Effects of Early Intervention on Cognitive Function of Low Birth Weight Preterm Infants." *Journal of Pediatrics* 120(3): 350–359.

Brown, Susan L. 2002. "Child Well-Being in Cohabiting Families." In *Just Living Together: Implications of Cohabitation on Families, Children, and Social Policy*, Alan Booth and Ann C. Crouter, eds. Mahwah, NJ: Lawrence Erlbaum Associates.

Bureau of Justice Statistics. 2007. *Criminal Offenders Statistics.* Washington, DC: Bureau of Justice Statistics. http://www.ojp.usdoj.gov/bjs/crimoff .htm#prevalence (accessed July 29, 2008).

Bureau of Labor Statistics. 2006. *Selected NLSY97 Variables by Survey Round.* Washington, DC: Bureau of Labor Statistics, National Longitudinal Surveys. http://www.bls.gov/nls/handbook/2005/selvary97.pdf (accessed July 28, 2008).

———. 2008. *Consumer Price Index Research Series Using Current Methods: Questions and Answers.* Washington, DC: Bureau of Labor Statistics. http://www.bls.gov/cpi/cpirsqa.pdf (accessed July 25, 2008).

Cameron, Stephen V., and James J. Heckman. 1993. "The Nonequivalence of High School Equivalents." *Journal of Labor Economics* 11(1): 1–47.

Card, David, and Jesse Rothstein. 2005. "Racial Segregation and the Black-White Test Score Gap." NBER Working Paper 12078. Cambridge, MA: National Bureau of Economic Research.

Carlson, Marcia J., and Sara McLanahan. 2002. "Fragile Families, Father Involvement, and Public Policy." In *Handbook of Father Involvement: Multidisciplinary Perspectives,* Catherine S. Tamis-LeMonda and Natasha Cabrera, eds. Mahwah, NJ: Lawrence Erlbaum Associates, pp. 461–488.

Carneiro, Pedro, and James J. Heckman. 2003. "Human Capital Policy." IZA Discussion Paper No. 821. Bonn, Germany: Institute for the Study of Labor.

Chandra, Amitabh. 2003. "Is the Convergence in the Racial Wage Gap Illusory?" NBER Working Paper 9476. Cambridge, MA: National Bureau of Economic Research.

Child Trends and the Center for Human Resource Research (Child Trends). 1999. *NLSY97 Codebook Supplement, Main File Round 1: Appendix 9: Family Process and Adolescent Outcome Measures.* Washington, DC: U.S. Department of Labor, Bureau of Labor Statistics. http://www .nlsinfo.org/nlsy97/docs/97HTML00/97guide/app9pdf.pdf (accessed July 29, 2008).

Clayton, Obie, Ronald B. Mincy, and David Blankenhorn, eds. 2003. *Black Fathers in Contemporary Society: Strengths, Weaknesses, and Strategies for Change.* New York: Russell Sage Foundation.

Comer, James P. 2004. *Leave No Child Behind: Preparing Today's Youth for Tomorrow's World.* New Haven, CT: Yale University Press.

DeLeire, Thomas C., and Ariel Kalil. 2002. "Good Things Come in Threes: Single-Parent Multigenerational Family Structure and Adolescent Adjustment." *Demography* 39(2): 393–413.

DiNardo, John E., and Jörn-Steffen Pischke. 1997. "The Returns to Computer Use Revisited: Have Pencils Changed the Wage Structure Too?" *Quarterly Journal of Economics* 112(1): 291–303.

Dion, M. Robin. 2005. "Healthy Marriage Programs: Learning What Works." *Future of Children* 15(2): 139–156.

Dornbusch, Sanford M., Philip L. Ritter, P. Herbert Leiderman, Donald F. Roberts, and Michael J. Fraleigh. 1987. "The Relation of Parenting Style to Adolescent School Performance." *Child Development* 58(5): 1244–1257.

Duncan, Greg J. 2005. *Income and Child Well-Being.* Geary Lecture Series 34. Dublin, Ireland: Economic and Social Research Institute.

Duncan, Greg J., Aletha C. Huston, and Thomas S. Weisner. 2007. *Higher Ground: New Hope for the Working Poor and Their Children.* New York: Russell Sage Foundation.

Dunifon, Rachel, Greg J. Duncan, and Jeanne Brooks-Gunn. 2001. "As Ye Sweep, So Shall Ye Reap." *American Economic Review* 91(2):150–154.

Dunifon, Rachel, and Lori Kowaleski-Jones. 2002. "Who's in the House? Race Differences in Cohabitation, Single Parenthood, and Child Development." *Child Development* 73(4): 1249–1264.

Dynarski, Susan, and Judith Scott-Clayton. 2007. "College Grants on a Postcard: A Proposal for Simple and Predictable Federal Student Aid." Hamilton Project Discussion Paper 2007-01. Washington, DC: Brookings Institution.

Eccles, Jacquelynne S., Diane Early, Kari Fraser, Elaine Belansky, and Karen McCarthy. 1997. "The Relation of Connection, Regulation, and Support for Autonomy to Adolescents' Functioning." *Journal of Adolescent Research* 12(2): 263–286.

Eccles, Jacquelynne S., and Jennifer Appleton Gootman, eds. 2002. *Community Programs to Promote Youth Development.* Washington, DC: National Academies Press.

Eccles, Jacquelynne S., Carol Midgley, Allan Wigfield, Christy Miller Buchanan, David Reuman, Constance Flanagan, and Douglas Mac Iver. 1993. "Development during Adolescence: The Impact of Stage-Environment Fit on Young Adolescents' Experiences in Schools and in Families." *American Psychologist* 48(2): 90–101.

Edelman, Peter, Harry J. Holzer, and Paul Offner. 2006. *Reconnecting Disadvantaged Young Men*. Washington, DC: Urban Institute.

Edin, Kathryn, and Maria Kefalas. 2005. *Promises I Can Keep: Why Poor Women Put Motherhood before Marriage*. Berkeley, CA: University of California Press.

Ellwood, David T., and Jonathan Crane. 1990. "Family Change among Black Americans: What Do We Know?" *Journal of Economic Perspectives* 4(4): 65–84.

Ellwood, David T., and Christopher Jencks. 2004. "The Uneven Spread of Single-Parent Families: What Do We Know? Where Do We Look for Answers?" In *Social Inequality*, Kathryn M. Neckerman, ed. New York: Russell Sage Foundation, pp. 3–78.

Ellwood, David T., and Thomas J. Kane. 2000. "Who Is Getting a College Education? Family Background and the Growing Gaps in Enrollment." In *Securing the Future: Investing in Children from Birth to College*, Sheldon Danziger and Jane Waldfogel, eds. New York: Russell Sage Foundation, pp. 283–324.

Freeman, Richard B. 1996. "Why Do So Many Young American Men Commit Crimes and What Might We Do About It?" *Journal of Economic Perspectives* 10(1): 25–42.

Freeman, Richard B., and James L. Medoff. 1982. "Why Does the Rate of Youth Labor Force Activity Differ across Surveys?" In *The Youth Labor Market Problem: Its Nature, Causes, and Consequences*, Richard B. Freeman and David A. Wise, eds. Chicago: University of Chicago Press, pp. 75–114.

Fryer, Roland G. Jr., and Steven D. Levitt. 2004. "Understanding the Black-White Test Score Gap in the First Two Years of School." *Review of Economics and Statistics* 86(2): 447–464.

Furstenberg, Frank F. Jr., Thomas D. Cook, Jacquelynne S. Eccles, Glen H. Elder Jr., and Arnold Sameroff. 1999. *Managing to Make It: Urban Families and Adolescent Success*. Chicago: University of Chicago Press.

Garfinkel, Irwin, Sara McLanahan, Daniel R. Meyer, and Judith A. Seltzer. 1998. *Fathers Under Fire: The Revolution in Child Support Enforcement*. New York: Russell Sage Foundation.

Geronimus, Arline T., and Sanders Korenman. 1993. "The Socioeconomic Costs of Teenage Childbearing: Evidence and Interpretation." *Demography* 30(2): 281–290.

Gormley, William T. Jr., and Ted Gayer. 2005. "Promoting School Readiness in Oklahoma: An Evaluation of Tulsa's Pre-K Program." *Journal of Human Resources* 40(3): 533–558.

Graefe, Deborah Roempke, and Daniel T. Lichter. 1999. "Life Course Transitions of American Children: Parental Cohabitation, Marriage, and Single Motherhood." *Demography* 36(2): 205–217.

Greenberg, Mark, Danielle Ewen, and Hannah Matthews. 2006. *Using TANF for Early Childhood Programs*. Washington, DC: Center for Law and Social Policy.

Grogger, Jeff. 1997. "Market Wages and Youth Crime." NBER Working Paper 5983. Cambridge, MA: National Bureau of Economic Research.

Gruber, Jonathan. 2000. "Is Making Divorce Easier Bad for Children? The Long Run Implications of Unilateral Divorce." NBER Working Paper 7968. Cambridge, MA: National Bureau of Economic Research.

———, ed. 2001. *Risky Behavior among Youths: An Economic Analysis*. Cambridge, MA: National Bureau of Economic Research.

Haurin, R. Jean. 1992. "Patterns of Childhood Residence and the Relationship to Young Adult Outcomes." *Journal of Marriage and the Family* 54(4): 846–860.

Hauser, Robert M. 1997. "Indicators of High School Completion and Dropout." In *Indicators of Children's Well-Being*, Robert M. Hauser, Brett V. Brown, and William Prosser, eds. New York: Russell Sage Foundation, pp. 152–184.

Hauser, Robert M., and Min-Hsiung Huang. 1996. "Trends in Black-White Test-Score Differentials." Institute for Research on Poverty Discussion Paper No. 1110-96.

Haveman, Robert, and Barbara Wolfe. 1995. "The Determinants of Children's Attainments: A Review of Methods and Findings." *Journal of Economic Literature* 33(4): 1829–1878.

Hindelang, Michael J., Travis Hirschi, and Joseph G. Weis. 1981. *Measuring Delinquency*. Sage Library of Social Research, Vol. 123. Thousand Oaks, CA: Sage Publications.

Hoffman, Saul D., E. Michael Foster, and Frank F. Furstenberg Jr. 1993. "Reevaluating the Costs of Teenage Childbearing: Response to Geronimus and Korenman." *Demography* 30(2): 291–296.

Holzer, Harry J. 1996. *What Employers Want: Job Prospects for Less-Educated Workers*. New York: Russell Sage Foundation.

———. 2000. "Racial Differences in Labor Market Outcomes among Men." In *America Becoming: Racial Trends and Their Consequences*, Neil J. Smelser, William Julius Wilson, and Faith Mitchell, eds. Vol. 2. Washington, DC: National Academies Press.

———. 2006. "Testimony at the Meeting of the Equal Employment Opportunity Commission, April 19." Washington, DC: Urban Institute. http://www.urban.org/publications/900953.html (accessed August 4, 2008).

———. 2007. "Better Workers for Better Jobs: Improving Worker Advancement in the Low-Wage Labor Market." Hamilton Project Discussion Paper 2007-15. Washington, DC: Brookings Institution.

———. 2009. "Collateral Costs: Effects of Incarceration on Employment and Earnings among Young Workers." In *Do Prisons Make Us Safer? The Benefits and Costs of the Prison Boom*, Steven Raphael and Michael A. Stoll, eds. New York: Russell Sage Foundation, pp. 239–266.

Holzer, Harry J., and Karin Martinson. 2005. "Can We Improve Job Retention and Advancement among Low-Income Working Parents?" National Poverty Center Working Paper No. 05-10. Prepared for the Working Families Roundtable, hosted by the Urban Institute's Assessing the New Federalism project, held in Washington, DC, May 9–10.

Holzer, Harry J., and Paul Offner. 2006. "Trends in the Employment Outcomes of Young Black Men, 1979–2000." In *Black Males Left Behind*, Ronald B. Mincy, ed. Washington, DC: Urban Institute, pp. 11–38.

Holzer, Harry J., Paul Offner, and Elaine Sorensen. 2005. "Declining Employment among Young Black Less-Educated Men: The Role of Incarceration and Child Support." *Journal of Policy Analysis and Management* 24(2): 329–350.

Holzer, Harry J., Steven Raphael, and Michael A. Stoll. 2003. "Employment Barriers Facing Ex-Offenders." Presented at the Urban Institute Reentry Roundtable "Employment Dimensions of Reentry: Understanding the Nexus between Prisoner Reentry and Work," held in New York, May 19–20.

———. 2006. "Perceived Criminality, Criminal Background Checks, and the Racial Hiring Preferences of Employers." *Journal of Law and Economics* 49(2): 451–480.

Holzer, Harry J., Diane Whitmore Schanzenbach, Greg J. Duncan, and Jens Ludwig. 2007. *The Economic Costs of Poverty in the United States: Subsequent Effects of Children Growing Up Poor*. Washington, DC: Center for American Progress.

Hotz, V. Joseph, Susan Williams McElroy, and Seth G. Sanders. 1996. "The Impacts of Teenage Childbearing on the Mothers and the Consequences of Those Impacts for Government." In *Kids Having Kids: Economic Costs and Social Consequences of Teen Pregnancy*, Rebecca A. Maynard, ed. Washington, DC: Urban Institute, pp. 55–94.

Hotz, V. Joseph, and John Karl Scholz. 2001. "Measuring Employment and Income for Low-Income Populations with Administrative and Survey Data." In *Studies of Welfare Populations: Data Collection and Research Issues*, Michele Ver Ploeg, Robert A. Moffitt, and Constance F. Citro, eds. Washington, DC: National Academies Press, pp. 275–315.

Jacob, Brian A. 2002. "Where the Boys Aren't: Non-Cognitive Skills, Returns to School, and the Gender Gap in Higher Education." *Economics of Education Review* 21(6): 589–598.

James-Burdumy, Susanne, Mark Dynarski, Mary Moore, John Deke, Wendy Mansfield, and Carol Pistorino. 2005. *When Schools Stay Open Late: The National Evaluation of the 21st Century Community Learning Centers Program.* Final report. Washington, DC: U.S. Department of Education.

Jencks, Christopher, and Susan E. Mayer. 1990. "The Social Consequences of Growing Up in a Poor Neighborhood." In *Inner-City Poverty in the United States*, Laurence E. Lynn Jr. and Michael G.H. McGeary, eds. Washington, DC: National Academies Press, pp. 111–186.

Jencks, Christopher, and Meredith Phillips, eds. 1998. *The Black-White Test Score Gap.* Washington, DC: Brookings Institution.

Johnson, William R., and Derek Neal. 1998. "Basic Skills and the Black-White Earnings Gap." In *The Black-White Test Score Gap*, Christopher Jencks and Meredith Phillips, eds. Washington, DC: Brookings Institution, pp. 480–500.

Journal of Human Resources (JHR). 2001. "Special Issue on Early Results from the National Longitudinal Survey of Youth, 1997 Cohort." *Journal of Human Resources* 36(4): 627–822.

Joyce, Theodore J., Robert Kaestner, and Sanders Korenman. 2000. "The Effect of Pregnancy Intention on Child Development." *Demography* 37(1): 83–94.

Juhn, Chinhui. 1992. "Decline of Male Labor Market Participation: The Role of Declining Market Opportunities." *Quarterly Journal of Economics* 107(1): 79–121.

———. 2000. "Black-White Employment Differential in a Tight Labor Market." In *Prosperity for All? The Economic Boom and African Americans*, Robert Cherry and William M. Rodgers III, eds. New York: Russell Sage Foundation, pp. 88–109.

Juhn, Chinhui, and Simon Potter. 2006. "Changes in Labor Force Participation in the United States." *Journal of Economic Perspectives* 20(3): 27–46.

Kalil, Ariel, Michael S. Spencer, Susan J. Spieker, and Lewayne D. Gilchrist. 1998. "Effects of Family Living Arrangements and Quality of Relationships on the Mental Health of Low-Income Adolescent Mothers." *Family Relations* 47(4): 433–441.

Kamp Dush, Claire M., and Rachel Dunifon. 2007. "The Unexamined Stable Family: An Examination of Child Well-Being in Stable Single Parent Families." Paper presented at the Annual Meeting of the Population Association of America, held in New York, March 29–31.

Katz, Lawrence F., and David H. Autor. 1999. "Changes in the Wage Structure and Earnings Inequality." In *The Handbook of Labor Economics, Vol. 3A*,

Orley C. Ashenfelter and David Card, eds. Amsterdam, North-Holland, pp. 1463–1555.

Kirschenman, Joleen, and Kathryn M. Neckerman. 1991. "We'd Love to Hire Them But...." In *The Urban Underclass*, Christopher Jencks and Paul E. Peterson, eds. Washington, DC: Brookings Institution, pp. 203–232.

Kling, Jeffrey R., Jens Ludwig, and Lawrence F. Katz. 2005. "Neighborhood Effects on Crime for Female and Male Youth: Evidence from a Randomized Housing Voucher Experiment." *Quarterly Journal of Economics* 120(1): 87–130.

Korenman, Sanders, Robert Kaestner, and Theodore J. Joyce. 2001. "Unintended Pregnancy and the Consequences of Nonmarital Childbearing." In *Out of Wedlock: Causes and Consequences of Nonmarital Fertility*, Lawrence L. Wu and Barbara Wolfe, eds. New York: Russell Sage Foundation, pp. 259–286.

Kornfeld, Robert, and Howard S. Bloom. 1999. "Measuring Program Impacts on Earnings and Employment: Do Unemployment Insurance Wage Reports from Employers Agree with Surveys of Individuals?" *Journal of Labor Economics* 17(1): 168–197.

Krueger, Alan B. 1993. "How Computers Have Changed the Wage Structure: Evidence from Microdata, 1884–1989." *Quarterly Journal of Economics* 108(1): 33–60.

Lang, Kevin, and Michael Manove. 2006. "Education and Labor Market Discrimination." NBER Working Paper 12257. Cambridge, MA: National Bureau of Economic Research.

Lang, Kevin, and Jay L. Zagorsky. 2001. "Does Growing Up with a Parent Absent Really Hurt?" *Journal of Human Resources* 36(2): 253–273.

Lansford, Jennifer E., Rosario Ceballo, Antonia Abbey, and Abigail J. Stewart. 2001. "Does Family Structure Matter? A Comparison of Adoptive, Two-Parent Biological, Single-Mother, Stepfather and Stepmother Households." *Journal of Marriage and Family* 63(3): 840–851.

Laumann, Edward O., John H. Gagnon, Robert T. Michael, and Stuart Michaels. 1994. *The Social Organization of Sexuality: Sexual Practices in the United States*. Chicago: University of Chicago Press.

Lee, Valerie E., David T. Burkam, Herbert Zimiles, and Barbara Ladewski. 1994. "Family Structure and Its Effect on Behavioral and Emotional Problems in Young Adolescents." *Journal of Research on Adolescence* 4(3): 405–437.

Lerman, Robert I. 2002. *Should Government Promote Healthy Marriages?* Short Takes on Welfare Policy No. 5. Washington, DC: Urban Institute.

———. 2007. "Career-Focused Education and Training for Youth." In *Reshaping the American Workforce in a Changing Economy*, Harry J. Holzer and

Demetra Smith Nightingale, eds. Washington, DC: Urban Institute Press, pp. 41–90.

Lichter, Daniel T., Diane K. McLaughlin, George Kephart, and David J. Landry. 1992. "Race and the Retreat from Marriage: A Shortage of Marriageable Men?" *American Sociological Review* 57(6): 781–799.

Ludwig, Jens, and Isabel Sawhill. 2007. "Success by Ten: Intervening Early, Often, and Effectively in the Education of Young Children." Hamilton Project Discussion Paper 2007-02. Washington, DC: Brookings Institution.

Manning, Wendy D., and Kathleen A. Lamb. 2003. "Adolescent Well-Being in Cohabiting, Married, and Single-Parent Families." *Journal of Marriage and Family* 65(4): 876–893.

Manning, Wendy D., Pamela J. Smock, and Debarun Majumdar. 2004. "The Relative Stability of Cohabiting and Marital Unions for Children." *Population Research and Policy Review* 23(2): 135–159.

Mayer, Susan E. 1997. *What Money Can't Buy: Family Income and Children's Life Chances*. Cambridge, MA: Harvard University Press.

Maynard, Rebecca A., ed. 1996. *Kids Having Kids: Economic Costs and Social Consequences of Teen Pregnancy*. Washington, DC: Urban Institute.

McKernan, Signe-Mary, and Caroline Ratcliffe. 2007. "The Effect of Welfare and IDA Policies on Asset Holdings." Paper presented at the University of Kentucky Center for Poverty Research conference "Ten Years After: Evaluating the Long-Term Effects of Welfare Reform on Children, Families, Welfare, and Work," held in Lexington, KY, April 12–13.

McLanahan, Sara. 1997. "Parent Absence or Poverty: Which Matters More?" In *Consequences of Growing Up Poor*, Greg J. Duncan and Jeanne Brooks-Gunn, eds. New York: Russell Sage Foundation, pp. 35–48.

———. 2004. "Diverging Destinies: How Children Are Faring under the Second Demographic Transition." *Demography* 41(4): 607–627.

McLanahan, Sara, and Lynne Casper. 1995. "Growing Diversity and Inequality in the American Family." In *State of the Union: America in the 1990s*, Reynolds Farley, ed. Vol. 2, *Social Trends*. New York: Russell Sage Foundation, pp. 1–45.

McLanahan, Sara, and Gary Sandefur. 1994. *Growing Up With a Single Parent: What Hurts, What Helps*. Cambridge MA: Harvard University Press.

Mead, Sara. 2006. *The Truth about Boys and Girls*. Washington, DC: Education Sector.

Meyer, Bruce D., and Dan T. Rosenbaum. 2001. "Welfare, the Earned Income Tax Credit, and the Labor Supply of Single Mothers." *Quarterly Journal of Economics* 116(3): 1063–1114.

Michael, Robert T., ed. 2001. *Social Awakening: Adolescent Behavior as Adulthood Approaches*. New York: Russell Sage Foundation.

Miller, Cynthia, and Virginia Knox. 2001. *The Challenge of Helping Low-Income Fathers Support Their Children: Final Lessons from Parents' Fair Share.* New York: MDRC.

Mincy, Ronald B, ed. 1994. *Nurturing Young Black Males.* Washington, DC: Urban Institute.

Mincy, Ronald B., and Elaine J. Sorensen. 1998. "Deadbeats and Turnips in Child Support Reform." *Journal of Policy Analysis and Management* 17(1): 44–51.

Mishel, Lawrence, and Joydeep Roy. 2006. *Rethinking High School Graduation Rates and Trends.* Washington, DC: Economic Policy Institute.

Moffitt, Robert A. 2001. "Welfare Benefits and Female Headship in U.S. Time Series." In *Out of Wedlock: Causes and Consequences of Nonmarital Fertility*, Lawrence L. Wu and Barbara Wolfe, eds. New York: Russell Sage Foundation, pp. 143–172.

Moore, Mignon R. 2001. "Family Environment and Adolescent Sexual Debut in Alternative Household Structures." In *Social Awakening: Adolescent Behavior as Adulthood Approaches*, Robert T. Michael, ed. New York: Russell Sage Foundation, pp. 109–136.

Morris, Pamela A., Lisa A. Gennetian, and Greg J. Duncan. 2005. *Effects of Welfare and Employment Policies on Young Children: New Findings on Policy Experiments Conducted in the Early 1990s.* New York: MDRC.

Morrison, Donna Ruane, and Andrew J. Cherlin. 1995. "The Divorce Process and Young Children's Well-Being: A Prospective Analysis." *Journal of Marriage and the Family* 57(3): 800–812.

National Campaign to Prevent Teen and Unplanned Pregnancy. 2008. *What Works: Curriculum-Based Programs That Prevent Teen Pregnancy.* Washington, DC: National Campaign to Prevent Teen and Unplanned Pregnancy.

Neal, Derek. 2005. "Why Has Black-White Skill Convergence Stopped?" NBER Working Paper W11090. Cambridge, MA: National Bureau of Economic Research.

Offner, Paul. 2002. "What's Love Got to Do With It? Why Oprah's Still Single: Society and Opportunities for African American People." *Washington Monthly* 34(3): 15–19.

Ooms, Theodora. 2007. *Adapting Healthy Marriage Programs for Disadvantaged and Culturally Diverse Populations: What Are the Issues?* CLASP Policy Brief No. 10. Washington, DC: Center for Law and Social Policy.

Ooms, Theodora, Jacqueline Boggess, Anne Menard, Mary Myrick, Paula Roberts, Jack Tweedie, and Pamela Wilson. 2006. *Building Bridges between Healthy Marriage, Responsible Fatherhood, and Domestic Violence Programs.* Washington, DC: National Conference of State Legislators and the Center for Law and Social Policy.

Orfield, Gary, ed. 2004. *Dropouts in America: Confronting the Graduation Rate Crisis*. Cambridge MA: Harvard Education Press.

Osterman, Paul. 2007. "Employment and Training Policies: New Directions for Less-Skilled Adults." In *Reshaping the American Workforce in a Changing Economy,* Harry J. Holzer and Demetra Smith Nightingale, eds. Washington, DC: Urban Institute, pp 119–154.

Page, Marianne E., and Ann Huff Stevens. 2005. "Understanding Racial Differences in the Economic Costs of Growing Up in a Single-Parent Family." *Demography* 42(1): 75–90.

Pager, Devah. 2003. "The Mark of a Criminal Record." *American Journal of Sociology* 108(5): 937–975.

———. 2007. *Marked: Race, Crime, and Finding Work in an Era of Mass Incarceration.* Chicago: University of Chicago Press.

Painter, Gary, and David I. Levine. 2000. "Family Structure and Youths' Outcomes: Which Correlations Are Causal?" *Journal of Human Resources* 35(3): 524–549.

Pennington, Hilary. 2006. Moderator of the Center for American Progress symposium "A Federal Role in Closing the Graduation Gap: Solutions for Resolving the Disparity in Graduation Rates," held in Washington, DC, November 17.

Pierret, Charles R. 2001. "The Effect of Family Structure on Youth Outcomes in the NLSY97." In *Social Awakening: Adolescent Behavior as Adulthood Approaches,* Robert T. Michael, ed. New York: Russell Sage Foundation, pp. 25–48.

Pirog, Maureen A., and Kathleen M. Ziol-Guest. 2006. "Child Support Enforcement: Programs and Policies, Impacts and Questions." *Journal of Policy Analysis and Management* 25(4): 943–990.

Primus, Wendell. 2006. "Improving Public Policies to Increase the Income and Employment of Low-Income Nonresident Fathers." In *Black Males Left Behind*, Ronald B. Mincy, ed. Washington, DC: Urban Institute, pp. 226–237.

Raphael, Steven. 2007. "Early Incarceration Spells and the Transition to Adulthood." In *The Price of Independence: The Economics of Early Adulthood*, Sheldon Danziger and Cecilia Elena Rouse, eds. New York: Russell Sage Foundation, pp. 278–306.

Raphael, Steven, and Michael A. Stoll. 2007. "Why Are So Many Americans in Prison?" Discussion Paper No. 1328–07. Madison, WI: Institute for Research on Poverty.

Rodgers, William M. III, and William E. Spriggs. 1996. "What Does the AFQT Really Measure? Race, Wages, Schooling, and the AFQT Score." *Review of Black Political Economy* 24(4): 13–46.

Rosenzweig, Mark R., and Kenneth I. Wolpin. 1993. Maternal Expectations and Ex Post Rationalizations: The Usefulness of Survey Information on the Wantedness of Children." *Journal of Human Resources* 28(2): 205–229.

Sameroff, Arnold J., Ronald Seifer, and W. Todd Bartko.1997. "Environmental Perspectives on Adaptation during Childhood and Adolescence." In *Developmental Psychopathology: Perspectives on Adjustments, Risk, and Disorder,* Suniya S. Luthar, Jacob A. Burack, Dante Cicchetti, and John R. Weisz, eds. New York: Cambridge University Press, pp. 507–526.

Sampson, Robert J., Stephen W. Raudenbush, and Felton Earls. 1997. "Neighborhoods and Violent Crime: A Multilevel Study of Collective Efficacy." *Science* 277(5328): 918–924.

Sandefur, Gary D., and Thomas Wells. 1999. "Does Family Structure Really Influence Educational Attainment?" *Social Science Research* 28(4): 331–357.

Schumacher, Rachel. 2003. *Family Support and Parent Involvement in Head Start: What Do Head Start Program Performance Standards Require?* Washington, DC: Center for Law and Social Policy.

Sigle-Rushton, Wendy, and Sara McLanahan. 2004. "Father Absence and Child Well-Being: A Critical Review." In *The Future of the Family*, Daniel P. Moynihan, Timothy M. Smeeding, and Lee Rainwater, eds. New York: Russell Sage Foundation, pp. 116–155.

Slicker, Ellen K. 1998. "Relationship of Parenting Style to Behavioral Adjustment in Graduating High School Seniors." *Journal of Youth and Adolescence* 27(3): 345–372.

Stark, Philip B. 1999. "Sampling to Adjust the U.S. Census." Miller Institute for Basic Research in Science Lunchtime Colloquium, Department of Statistics, University of California, Berkeley, January 12.

Steinberg, Laurence, Susie D. Lamborn, Sanford M. Dornbusch, and Nancy Darling. 1992. "Impact of Parenting Practices on Adolescent Achievement: Authoritative Parenting, School Involvement, and Encouragement to Succeed." *Child Development* 63(5): 1266–1281.

Stevenson, Betsey, and Justin Wolfers. 2007. "Marriage and Divorce: Changes and Their Driving Forces." NBER Working Paper 12944. Cambridge, MA: National Bureau of Economic Research.

Swanson, Christopher B. 2004. *Who Graduates? Who Doesn't? A Statistical Portrait of Public High School Graduation, Class of 2001.* Washington, DC: Urban Institute.

Tepper, Robin L. 2001. "Parental Regulation and Adolescent Discretionary Time-Use Decisions: Findings from the NLSY97." In *Social Awakening: Adolescent Behavior as Adulthood Approaches*, Robert T. Michael, ed. New York: Russell Sage Foundation, pp. 79–105.

Thomas, Adam, and Isabel Sawhill. 2002. "For Richer or for Poorer: Marriage as an Antipoverty Strategy." *Journal of Policy Analysis and Management* 21(4): 587–599.

Tucker, M. Belinda, and Claudia Mitchell-Kernan, eds. 1995. *The Decline in Marriage among African Americans: Causes, Consequences, and Policy Implications*. New York: Russell Sage Foundation.

Turner, Margery Austin, Susan J. Popkin, and Lynette A. Rawlings, eds. 2008. *Public Housing and the Legacy of Segregation*. Washington, DC: Urban Institute.

Turner, Sarah. 2007. "Higher Education Policies Generating the 21st Century Workforce." In *Reshaping the American Workforce in a Changing Economy*, Harry J. Holzer and Demetra Smith Nightingale, eds. Washington, DC: Urban Institute, pp. 91–116.

Viscusi, W. Kip. 1986. "Market Incentives for Criminal Behavior." In *The Black Youth Employment Crisis*, Richard B. Freeman and Harry J. Holzer, eds. Chicago: University of Chicago Press, pp. 301–352.

Waite, Linda J., and Maggie Gallagher. 2000. *The Case for Marriage: Why Married People Are Happier, Healthier, and Better Off Financially*. New York: Random House.

Waldfogel, Jane. 1998. "Understanding the 'Family Gap' in Pay for Women with Children." *Journal of Economic Perspectives* 12(1): 137–156.

———. 2007. "Work-Family Policies." In *Reshaping the American Workforce in a Changing Economy*, Harry J. Holzer and Demetra Smith Nightingale, eds. Washington, DC: Urban Institute, pp 273–292.

Weiner, David A., Byron F. Lutz, and Jens Ludwig. 2006. "The Effects of School Desegregation on Crime." Paper presented at the 2007 Allied Social Science Association meetings, held in Chicago, January 5–7.

Western, Bruce. 2006. *Punishment and Inequality in America*. New York: Russell Sage Foundation.

Wilson, William Julius. 1987. *The Truly Disadvantaged: The Inner City, the Underclass, and Public Policy*. Chicago: University of Chicago Press.

———. 1996. *When Work Disappears: The World of the New Urban Poor*. New York: Alfred A. Knopf.

Wu, Lawrence L., and Barbara Wolfe, eds. 2001. *Out of Wedlock: Causes and Consequences of Nonmarital Fertility*. New York: Russell Sage Foundation.

The Authors

Carolyn J. Hill is an associate professor of public policy at Georgetown University. She received her MA in public policy analysis in 1996 from the La Follette Institute at the University of Wisconsin–Madison and her PhD in 2001 from the Harris Graduate School of Public Policy Studies at the University of Chicago.

Hill's research focuses on whether and why public programs are effective, and how they can be improved. She is the author of *Improving Governance: A New Logic for Empirical Research* (with Laurence E. Lynn Jr. and Carolyn J. Heinrich, Georgetown University Press 2002) and *Public Management: A Three-Dimensional Approach* (with Laurence E. Lynn Jr., CQ Press 2008). Her work has been published in the *Journal of Public Administration Research and Theory*, the *Journal of Policy Analysis and Management*, the *Review of Economics and Statistics*, *Health Services Research*, and the *Journal of Research on Educational Effectiveness*.

Harry J. Holzer is a professor of public policy at Georgetown University and a senior fellow at the Urban Institute in Washington, DC. He is a former chief economist for the U.S. Department of Labor and a former professor of economics at Michigan State University. He received his BA from Harvard in 1978 and his PhD in economics from Harvard in 1983. He is a senior affiliate of the National Poverty Center at the University of Michigan and a research affiliate of the Institute for Research on Poverty at the University of Wisconsin–Madison. He is also a nonresident senior fellow with the Brookings Metropolitan Policy Program and a member of the editorial board at the *Journal of Policy Analysis and Management*.

Holzer's research has focused primarily on the labor market problems of low-wage workers and other disadvantaged groups. His books include *The Black Youth Employment Crisis* (coedited with Richard Freeman, University of Chicago Press 1986), *What Employers Want: Job Prospects for Less-Educated Workers* (Russell Sage Foundation 1996), *Employers and Welfare Recipients: The Effects of Welfare Reform in the Workplace* (with Michael Stoll, Public Policy Institute of California 2001), *Moving Up or Moving On: Who Advances in the Low-Wage Labor Market* (with Fredrik Andersson and Julia Lane, Russell Sage Foundation 2005), *Reconnecting Disadvantaged Young Men* (with Peter Edelman and Paul Offner, Urban Institute Press 2006), and *Reshaping the American Workforce in a Changing Economy* (coedited with Demetra Smith Nightingale, Urban Institute Press 2007).

Henry Chen is a research associate at Harvard Business School. He received his BA from Northwestern University in 2003. From 2003 to 2007 he was a Research Associate at the Urban Institute. His research has focused on the personal finance, employment, and education patterns of low-income families and other disadvantaged groups.

Index

The italic letters *f*, *n*, and *t* following a page number indicate that the subject information of the heading is within a figure, note, or table, respectively, on that page. Double italics indicate multiple but consecutive elements.

Armed Services Vocational Aptitude
Battery (ASVAB)
gender differences in scores on, 32,
66*t*, 74, 77*t*, 102*t*
household characteristics and, 107,
146*t*–53*t*
household structure and, 70, 74, 75,
79*t*, 80, 81*t*, 105
NLSY data from, 14, 26, 33*t*, 49*n*10,
112*t*–13*t*
percentile as predictor of employment
outcome, 41*t*, 46*t*, 75, 79*t*, 140*t*,
142*t*
sibling fixed effects on, 80, 81*t*
Associate's degree. *See* College degrees
ASVAB. *See* Armed Services Vocational
Aptitude Battery
Attitudes, 11, 74
parents and, 9, 85
role models and, 6, 9
youth, and employment, 14, 20*n*2

Bachelor's degree. *See* College degrees
BJS. *See* Bureau of Justice Statistics
Black youth. *See* African American youth
BLS. *See* Bureau of Labor Statistics
Boys and Girls Clubs of America, youth
development, 133
Breast-feeding, effect on children, 8
Bureau of Justice Statistics (BJS),
incarceration data, 24–25, 37
Bureau of Labor Statistics (BLS), 25,
48*n*6, 90, 116*n*1
Bush, Pres. George W., marriage
promotion, 128

Careers, as disadvantage offset, 132,
136*n*2
Carolina Abecedarian Project, 131–132
Caucasian youth, 6
education and employment of, 146*t*–
47*t*
men and, 4, 20*n*1
women and, 40*t*–42*t*, 76*t*, 77*t*
(*see also* Caucasian youth,
minorities *vs.*)

household structures for, 57, 58*t*,
59–60, 61*t*, 72*ff*–73*ff*
family income and, 59*t*, 62*t*–68*t*,
69
minorities *vs.*
educational attainment of, 5, 18,
31*t*, 33*t*, 74, 77*t*, 86*n*15
employment of, 18, 28–30
mothers of, 60, 86*n*12
risky behaviors by gender, 34*t*, 36*t*,
78*t*
wages of, 146*t*–47*t*
gender and, 28–30, 29*t*, 76*t*
racial gap and, 4–5, 20*n*3, 84,
112*t*–13*t*
Center for Employment Opportunities
(CEO), New York, 137*n*5
Child care, provision of, 28, 130, 133
Child support enforcement
labor market activity and, 4, 21*n*13
policy implications involving, 129,
134–135
as predictor of unwed birth, 20–21*n*8
Child Trends (research center), 21*n*16
Childhood, 8
education during, 5, 32, 131–133
household structures during, 53, 144*t*
Cigarette use. *See* Smoking
CIP. *See* Consumer Price Index
Cohabitation. *See* Nonmarried-
cohabitation households
College degrees
by gender and race, 31*t*, 41*t*, 46*t*, 74,
77*t*, 101*t*
mothers of 12-year-olds with, 60, 61*t*,
80–82, 81*t*
predictors of, 30, 49–50*n*19, 75, 79*t*
time to earn, 30, 49–50*n*19
College enrollment, 132
associated characteristics with, 110,
112*t*–13*t*, 117*nn*9–10
as educational outcome measure, 1,
25, 74, 75, 77*t*, 79*t*, 101*t*, 146*t*–53*t*
employment regressions and, 140*t*–43*t*
minority women and, 5, 18
school types for, 25–26, 30, 130

About the Institute

The W.E. Upjohn Institute for Employment Research is a nonprofit research organization devoted to finding and promoting solutions to employment-related problems at the national, state, and local levels. It is an activity of the W.E. Upjohn Unemployment Trustee Corporation, which was established in 1932 to administer a fund set aside by Dr. W.E. Upjohn, founder of The Upjohn Company, to seek ways to counteract the loss of employment income during economic downturns.

The Institute is funded largely by income from the W.E. Upjohn Unemployment Trust, supplemented by outside grants, contracts, and sales of publications. Activities of the Institute comprise the following elements: 1) a research program conducted by a resident staff of professional social scientists; 2) a competitive grant program, which expands and complements the internal research program by providing financial support to researchers outside the Institute; 3) a publications program, which provides the major vehicle for disseminating the research of staff and grantees, as well as other selected works in the field; and 4) an Employment Management Services division, which manages most of the publicly funded employment and training programs in the local area.

The broad objectives of the Institute's research, grant, and publication programs are to 1) promote scholarship and experimentation on issues of public and private employment and unemployment policy, and 2) make knowledge and scholarship relevant and useful to policymakers in their pursuit of solutions to employment and unemployment problems.

Current areas of concentration for these programs include causes, consequences, and measures to alleviate unemployment; social insurance and income maintenance programs; compensation; workforce quality; work arrangements; family labor issues; labor-management relations; and regional economic development and local labor markets.

Printed in the United States
141636LV00003B/2/P